Your Sperm Won!

Experiencing Your Value

As A Championship Human Being!

(A Victorious Secret Book)

Steve Simms

ALE

Attitude-Lifter Enterprises

2720 Hillsboro Road, Brentwood, TN 37027

ISBN: 0-964821 0-1-X

Cover design by Jim York

Attitude-Lifter Enterprises
2720 Hillsboro Road
Brentwood, Tennessee 37027

PRINTED IN THE UNITED STATES OF AMERICA

CONTENTS

You're A Winner; Here's The Proof; We're Not Talking
Pride; We're Talking Value; What About Yourself?; Cousin
Joe's Story; A Trip To A Casino; Joan's Not Alone; What's
The Problem; Feeling Or Facts; The Floor Is Moving; The
Victorious Secret; Why Believe The Truth About Yourself?;
Where Did You Get Your Beliefs?; Seven Steps To Change A
False Or Ineffective Belief; Which Comes First–Chicken Or
The Egg?

Do You Know who You Are?; What's A Power Acrostic?;
Success–You Were Born With It; Probability–You Beat All
The Odds; Experience–You Have Awareness; Reality–You
Are A Fact; Miracle–You Are One; Everybody–You're Part
Of A Family Of Winners; Gratitude–Appreciate Your Value,
Growth–Go Ahead And Be What You Already Are.

You Have Value To Others; You Have Value Because Of
Your Service; You Have Value Because You Are Alive; You
Have Value Because You Were Created; You Have Value
Because You Are One Of A Kind; You Have Value Because
You Have Ability; You Have Value Because You Are Free;
Do You See What You Are Worth?; Abraham Lincoln's
Advice.

Turn Worry Into Worglee; Get Your Hopes Up With Worglee; A Boy And A Girl; Do Worglee—Be Happy.

DEDICATION

To all the championship human beings
Who don't feel like winners.
May these ideas
Help you to feel
Like the world class person
That you are!

Steve Simms

ACKNOWLEDGEMENTS

Thank you to my wife, Ernie, who repeatedly encouraged me to write a second book and backed up her encouragement by helping me throughout the project. Without her this book wouldn't have been written.

Thank you to my daughter, Amelia, for her inspiration.

Thank you to my proof readers and amazing supporters–family and friend who came through when I needed them: Dot Simms, Charlie Simms, Ernie Simms, and Charles Newbold.

Thank you to Joe Walker for sharing the story about his discovery of an unknown half-aunt. Joe didn't realize it, but that story got me thinking about a championship sperm and an incredible egg.

Thank you to Historic Rugby, Tennessee for letting me use the Thomas Hughes Library.

Thank you to Jim York for his work on the cover and to May Person for typesetting the manuscript.

Thank you to the Sunday night group for all your prayers, support, and encouragement.

Thank you to Dale and Melanie Jackson for their friendship and encouragement through the years and to Melanie for the illustration to go with my poem, "What Makes A Champion."

Steve Simms

"Too many people overvalue what they are not and undervalue what they are."
Malcolm Forbes

"I've always seen myself as a winner, even as a kid. If I hadn't, I just might have gone down the drain a couple of times."
Truman Capote

Steve Simms

What Makes A Champion?
by Steve Simms

What does it take
To be a champion?
A first place medal
In the Olympics?
A contract
For several million dollars?
The winning score
In the world championship game?
Unrivaled fame and fortune?

Don't underrate yourself.
For you have achieved
The greatest prize
The privilege to be alive.

Against impossible odds
In secret places
Through hundreds
Of generations
The formula for you
Overcoming
Overwhelming obstacles
Amazingly won its way
To the day
You were formed.

What does it take
To be a champion?
A breath to breathe,
A mind to think,
A heart to care,
One life to live.

Steve Simms

"Life is precious and extraordinary. Put your attention on this fact and little, ordinary things will take on a whole new meaning."

Richard Carlson

"It came to me that having life itself, life being such a miraculous achievement, is like winning the grand prize. What we do after that—what we do with our lives—is the frosting on the cake."

Earl Nightingale

"You are somebody!"

Jesse Jackson

Chapter 1

Championship Sperm Meets Incredible Egg, Makes Winner

You're A Winner

THE WORLD IS FULL of winners, championship human beings, who are walking around the planet, feeling, thinking, talking and acting like losers! If you are reading these words, then you are a world championship human being.

I know you may seldom feel like a winner. In fact, at this very moment you may be feeling like a dog, thinking like a log, and acting in a fog; but none-the-less, you are a world class person and I can prove it!

Here's The Proof

At the moment you came into existence, there were about 400 million other human beings who could have been conceived, but your sperm won the right to unite with your egg! You've been a winner since day one (or day minus nine months, if you prefer) because you came from a championship sperm and an incredible egg. (When I told a friend, Nancy, about this, she said, "I never before realized I had a sperm.")

That's right, your sperm won, you tremendously lucky individual. You beat one in 400 million odds! That's pretty impressive, isn't it? But we're just getting started. Before you finish this book you will know you are of infinite value. You will feel so good about yourself that you will want to jump up and click your heels together and yell "yeeee-haaaa!"–all day long!

We're Not Talking Pride

Now I'm not talking about pride. Pride is based on comparing yourself to other people. Pride wants to be better than everybody else, number one in the world, and that's a very difficult goal. Of all the billions of folks alive in the world, there is only one smartest, only one richest, only one who can run the fastest, jump the highest, swim the longest distance, and only one for every other category in *Guiness Book of World Records!*

Let's face it, your chances of being the best on the planet are slim. Sure, you may become a legend in your own mind, but for you to be the verifiable best is not very likely. Pride is a dead end street. That's why Emily Bronte said: "Proud people breed sorrows for themselves." And Solomon said: "Pride goes before destruction." Harold Coffin put it this way: "Staring up to admire your own halo, creates a pain in the neck."

We're Talking Value

This book is not about pride! It is about value—your value as a human being. And your value is not based on how well you compare to others. The source of your value, as we will discover in this book, is far more powerful, stable, and secure than any comparison to other people, because your sperm won. You beat those one in 400 million odds.

But we are just getting started exploring your value. Let me use myself as an example. My mother came from Mississippi and my dad from Texas. What were the odds of their meeting? And even if they met, what were the odds that they would like each other? (They have both met thousands of people whom they didn't have children with.) And even if they got married and decided to have kids, what are the odds that my incredible egg would have been waiting for my championship sperm at precisely the right moment? Pretty slim, I'd say. Don't you think it is amazing that I'm alive? If another egg had been there another human being would have been conceived and I would have never come into existence.

What About Yourself?

If your mother and father hadn't met, your sperm wouldn't have even been in the race! And you would never have been in the human race!

And what if the sperm that became your mother had never met the egg that became your mother? Where would you be then? Or what if the egg that became your father had never met the sperm that became your father? No you in that case, either!

What about your grandparents, great-grandparents, great-great, great-great-great, and all the way up your family tree? If only one tiny sperm in your entire family tree had lost its race or if only one egg had not been in the proper place at the proper time, then you would be nothing!

What are the odds that you (Put your name here _____,) would be born on this planet? I can't even conceive (excuse the pun) of a number that large. You are a mathematical impossibility! The odds are so great against your conception, that you couldn't have happened. Your existence is impossible! And yet here you are, reading this book!

You incredible odds breaker! You unfathomable winner! Your sperm won! You are a statistical miracle!

Cousin Joe's Story

My cousin, Joe, shared this story with me. After his father died, Joe learned that his paternal grandfather had been married before he had married Joe's grandmother and had another family. Joe did some research and found out he had an elderly half-aunt still living. So he went to visit her.

Joe told his aunt that her father was his grandfather and asked her about her memories of him. Joe's aunt told him that she still remembered her father kissing her, then mounting a horse and riding away, never to return, when she was five years old.

As she described her grief Joe couldn't keep the tears out of his eyes. He found himself wishing his grandfather had never abandoned his first family. As he left his aunt and walked back to the car, reality hit him like a bolt of lightning. "Wait a minute!" Joe thought to himself. "If my grandfather hadn't left his first family and married my grandmother, I wouldn't be here now to feel sorry for my half-aunt!" Joe got a glimpse of the odds that he beat to be on our planet. He realized how incredibly lucky he was to have been born!

A Trip To A Casino

Meet Joan. I made her up. Joan walks into the Luxor Casino in Las Vegas to play the slots. She plays the maximum play on the first slot machine, spins the wheels, and hits the largest jackpot.

She moves over to the second one and does the same. Then the third, fourth, and so on, until she plays all 2,400 slots in the Luxor Casino and wins the maximum jackpot on each one. The casino is in shambles. There are TV cameras, reporters, and hundreds of cheering and ecstatic onlookers.

But Joan is oblivious to it all. She mopes over to the bar, sits down and starts to sob, and says over and over: "I'm such a loser! I'm pathetic! I'm so unlucky!"

What do you think about Joan? "She's nuts!" Right? Of course, Joan's nuts. She's done the impossible! Most people would think her luck is the greatest example of luck in the history of the world and yet she still thinks she is a loser. It's absurd!

Joan's Not Alone

Every human being who has ever been born is far luckier than Joan! (For your sperm to win the right to your incredible egg, you had to beat even greater odds than Joan did!) Nevertheless billions of people complain about what losers they are! It's absurd!

The man in bankruptcy court is a bigger winner than Joan! The woman with the broken heart is a bigger winner than Joan! The homeless individual sleeping under the bridge and smelling like a sewer is a bigger winner than Joan! The hospital patient is a bigger winner than Joan! The person on welfare is a bigger winner than Joan! The crime victim is a bigger winner than Joan! The drug addict is a bigger winner than Joan! The athlete cut from the team is a bigger winner

9

than Joan! The guy in the jail cell is a bigger winner than Joan! And you, too, (Yes you!) are a bigger winner than Joan!

And yet many of these winners are sobbing, complaining and grumbling about life. Like Joan, many of life's winners have become whiners—you might even call them whine-o's! They have entered miraculously into life's restaurant and asked for the "whine list" instead of life's fine wine list. It's absurd! Like Barbara Gordon said: "Others may argue about whether the world ends with a bang or a whimper. I just want to make sure mine doesn't end with a whine."

What's The Problem

So what, if Joan says: "I'm such a loser! I'm pathetic! I'm so unlucky!" She can whine until the Luxor accountants count all her money and the IRS takes its share, but she won't change a thing! Joan's a winner whether she feels like it or not!

The facts dispute Joan's feelings. She may feel like a loser. She may say she is a loser. She may think she is a loser. She may act like a loser and even convince some people of her loser status. But it "just ain't so!"

Joan is completely out of touch with reality! She may as well think she is Napoleon or Princess Di! As Demosthenes said: "Nothing is easier than self-deceit." Deceit is to believe a lie. Most of the people on our planet choose to believe the lie that tells them they are not champions rather than the truth that says they are! Why is self-deceit so easy for us?

Feelings Or Facts

Deceit comes easily because our feelings are often false! Feelings are not a reliable gauge of reality! Did you ever feel like everybody forgot your birthday? Maybe all day long you felt hurt and rejected by your family, friends, and co-workers. Then when you opened the door of your home that night, a room full of people shouted with love and enthusiasm: "Surprise! Happy Birthday!"

You wasted a day listening to lying feelings and proved my point that feelings are not facts! You genuinely felt unloved and forgotten, when in reality you were being loved a lot that day.

The Floor Is Moving!

Let me give you another example. Wherever you are reading this book, does it feel like the floor (or the ground) is moving? If you answer yes, you may be on too strong a medication, because floors and the ground normally don't seem to be moving.

Let me ask you a question. Do you believe the floor in your home is moving? Think about it! When I ask groups of people this question in my speeches and seminars, 80% or more will raise their hand to indicate they do not believe the floor is moving. They answered and voted according to their feelings.

But what about the facts? It is an indisputable fact that the entire earth is a large ball spinning in space. If you are anywhere on the surface of our planet, you are moving in a circle, making one complete rotation every 24 hours. Not only that, your floor is flying through space on its yearly journey around the sun.

After reminding people of the facts, almost everybody (except The Flat Earth Society) will finally agree with me that the floor is indeed moving. They make a conscious choice to believe the facts rather than their feelings. That is life's victorious secret.

The Victorious Secret

You can begin to personally experience your value as a championship human being when you choose to believe the facts about your life rather than believing the false feelings you have about yourself! Life will become a victorious celebration for you as you set aside fickle feelings and discover fabulous facts! As Ellen Sue Stern said: "Believing in our hearts that who we are is enough, is the key to a more satisfying and balanced life."

You may feel like a loser. Or you may just feel like you are average. But the truth is you are spectacular. Col. WM. C. Hunter said: "When the atmosphere gets blue, and you feel miserable, don't give way to your feelings, but get out your mental brush and dip it in the pot of courage, and with the rosy paint, blot out the blue spots."

My goal in this book is two-fold: 1) To demonstrate and prove that you are magnificent. And 2) To help you to fully believe it so that it becomes a personal experience for you. Benjamin Disraeli said: "The greatest good you can do for another is not just to share your riches, but to reveal to him his own."

Why Believe The Truth About Yourself?

More than any other factor, what you believe about yourself and your life, influences what you experience in life. Oprah Winfrey has said: "You are what you are by what you believe." William J.H. Boetcker said: "Your success depends mainly upon what you think of yourself and whether you believe in yourself." Wally Amos said: "It is so important to believe in yourself. Believe that you can do it, under any circumstances. Because if you believe you can, then you really will."

Carol Sheffield said: "As our beliefs actually change, so do our experiences." And Judy Tatelbaum states the inverse: "We can be victimized by our beliefs." Mahatma Ghandi said: "If I believe I cannot do something, it makes me incapable of doing it. But when I believe I can, then I acquire the ability to do it even if I didn't have it in the beginning." Ask yourself: "What images have I put in place of reality?"

Where Did You Get Your Beliefs?

Since our beliefs are so important, we need to ask: "Where did we get our beliefs?" Most of us got our beliefs from two sources: 1) our feelings and 2) the people and society around us.

Bertrand Russell said: "Men tend to have the beliefs that suit their passions (feelings)." As we have seen, choosing to believe your feelings often leads to self-deceit.

Buddha said: "Do not believe in anything simply because you have heard it. . . Do not believe in anything because it is spoken and rumored by many. . . Do not believe merely on the authority of your teachers and elders." Unfortunately, many of us have accepted the beliefs around us without even questioning their truth or their practicality. We have blindly believed things that are false and things that are harmful to us.

You are a winner! You may not believe it because you don't feel it or because you were not taught it. Still it is true. You can more fully experience your value as a championship human being if you will do the following seven things: (Examples are in parenthesis.)

Seven Steps To Change A False Or Ineffective Belief

1) Discover your false or ineffective beliefs. As we discuss false and ineffective beliefs in this book, ask yourself

13

honestly, "Do I believe that?" Ask yourself: "What do I believe about myself and my life that is causing me pain or harm?" (Here are false beliefs: "You are a loser," or "You are average.")

2) Refuse to defend your false or ineffective beliefs. As you discover things you believe which are not helping you, do not make excuses. Don't be defensive in your own mind or in conversation with others. Admit the belief is wrong for you. Renounce it. (Say: "I am not a loser. I am not average.")

3) Decide in your mind and heart to change the belief no matter how long it takes. Fight the belief. Refuse to believe it or consider it or speak it any longer. Don't give in to feelings that tell you the old belief is true. Don't give up. It can take weeks, months, or even years to completely win the battle over a false belief. (Never say to yourself or anyone else that you are "a loser.")

4) Adopt a new belief in place of the old one. Write out a one sentence statement of the new belief. Memorize it. Repeat it over and over whether you feel it or not. (Write down: "I am a world championship human being!")

5) Research everything you can find to resist the old belief and to reinforce the new one. Read this book over and over. Read, listen to audio and video tapes that build you up. (Associate with people who encourage you. Disassociate as much as possible from people who put you down.)

6) Tell other people that your new belief about you is true. (Say to others: "I have finally learned to believe in myself!")

7) Act like your new belief is true! Pretend to believe in yourself whether you feel like it or not. (Pretend you are an actor playing the role of a championship human being.)

If you follow these seven steps, you can change any belief. You can (in a few weeks or months) learn to believe that you are a winner.

Which Comes First—Chicken Or Egg

Some people think they will believe they are a winner when they feel like one. That will never happen. Belief always precedes feeling. If you feel like a loser or like an average person, it is because you believe it to be so. If you want to feel better about yourself you have to believe better about yourself.

By following the steps above and by applying the other principles in this book, you can believe before you feel. Go ahead. Decide right now that you are going to feel great about you. Come on. Your sperm won the right to your egg. You're a bigger winner than slot-wonder Joan! As Michael de Montaigne said: "We are all of us richer than we think we are." Believe it!

Follow me into chapter two for an acrostic that can change your life.

Steve Simms

"There are no hopeless situations; there are only people who have grown hopeless about them."

Clare Booth Luce

"Self-understanding rather than self-condemnation is the way to inner peace."

Joshua Loth Liebman

Chapter 2

S P E R M - E G G Power-Acrostic

Do You Know Who You Are?

WHO ARE YOU? Most people answer that question with their name. I'm Bill, Mary, Joan, Joe, etc. Then they give their occupation: carpenter, doctor, plumber, CEO, lawyer, dentist, etc. But you are neither your name or your occupation.

To "know yourself" is some of the most important advice ever given. Jack H. Grossman said: "It is interesting that when people buy a pet, a plant, or any other living thing, they inquire about the nature as well as the care and feeding requirements of what they purchase. Yet many people go through life knowing less about themselves than about a plant or a pet."

Sidney J. Harris said: "Ninety percent of the world's woe comes from people not knowing themselves, their abilities, their frailties, even their real virtues. Most of us go almost all the way through life as complete strangers to ourselves."

Who are you? The goal of this book is to help answer that question. One word can never tell who you are. You are

17

too magnificent for such a simple description! So to help us out in our search for who you are I have developed the :
S P E R M - E G G Power Acrostic.

What's A Power Acrostic?

Success	You were born with it!
Probability	You beat all the odds!
Experience	You have awareness!
Reality	You are a fact!
Miracle	You are one!
Everybody	You're part of a family of winners!
Gratitude	You can appreciate!
Growth	You can become what you already are!

Success—You Were Born With It

From the moment you were born you have possessed the world's richest treasure. In fact, you brought it into the world with you. Nothing you ever accomplish in your life will be as valuable to you as this treasure. All the awards you ever win; all the money you ever make; all the goals you ever achieve; all the records you ever break; all the possessions you ever gather; will mean nothing to you when you have to give up your first treasure.

Every new born baby has it, custom made. Very few people would ever willingly give it up for any price. Yet in the effort to achieve so-called "success" many people forget all about the treasure that is their only true success! The world's greatest success and richest treasure is to possess and enjoy human life! Perhaps a baby does it best, taking in all the sights, sounds, and sensations for the very first time with an innocent delight. But the joys, pleasures, and curiosity of childhood are often put away by adolescents and adults.

We frequently forget about our natural born success and begin to climb the so-called, "ladder of success," to keep up with the Joneses, to make something out of ourselves. But nothing we can make out of ourselves in financial terms can ever hold a candle to what we already are: A BORN WINNER!

Probability—You Beat All The Odds

I've heard someone say the odds of our life-filled planet coming into existence are about the same odds as blowing up a printing factory and having all the debris accidentally turn into 10,000 sets of the Encyclopedia Britannica.

Lewis Thomas said: "Statistically, the probability of any one of us being here is so small that you'd think the mere fact of existing would keep us all in a contented dazzlement of surprise."

You are an odds-beater, someone who defied all the obstacles, all the impossibilities, in order to have your life. You are amazing. You are awesome! I think Henry David Thoreau had a glimpse of the statistical odds against his existence when he said: "I have never yet gotten over my surprise that I should have been born in the most estimable place in the world and in the very nick of time."

Experience—You Have Awareness

You have a mind and you know it! You feel the sun on your skin. You taste your food. You are in touch with your world. You think thoughts. You have feelings. You respond to your environment to make it better, more comfortable. When things don't go the way you want them to, you experience emotional pain. You care about other people.

You remember the past and you imagine the future that has yet to happen. You have consciousness. A rock knows nothing. A plant knows nothing. An animal knows hunger and pain and basic instincts but you know millions of experiences. They are stored in your memory banks. You are infinitely superior to all the life forms on the planet, because you are a conscious human being.

You are more than an object—more than a robot—more than an animal. You are a person—a personality! You are not just existing. You experience reality! You are aware.

Reality—You Are A Fact

You exist in reality. You are not a character in a story. You are not an illusion. You are not bits and bytes in a computer. You are real. As Joan Havoc said: "You are all you will ever have for certain."

You have a body that moves around the surface of our planet. But you are more than your body. You have thoughts, ideas, emotions that are not mere electrical impulses as some would have you believe, but are real.

The real you is more than physical. The real you cannot be explained only by material reality. The inner you is as real as your body. Your thoughts, opinions, and emotions matter. They are not incidentals. They are vital. Because the inner you is so real, great care should be given to your inward reality. Your thoughts, feelings, and opinions should be carefully selected.

Very few people are careless with their body. Few would lie down on a major highway in rush hour traffic. Few would stroll blindfolded on the edge of a 50 story rooftop. The reality of their physical body stops them.

Yet many people are careless with their thoughts, feelings, and opinions. They fail to see the reality of their inner world and their carelessness causes them great pain and self-destruction.

You exist not only physically, but also mentally and emotionally and spiritually.

Miracle—You Are One

Albert Einstein said: "There are two ways to live your life. One is as though nothing is a miracle. The other is as though everything is a miracle."

Once again you have a choice. You can choose to see yourself as a product of luck—the time and chance evolution of life according to natural laws.

You can choose to believe your family tree includes great-great-grandma monkey and great-great-grandpa dolphin all the way back to one-celled grannie amoeba. (You might even want to tell yourself that your amoeba won.)

Or you can choose to see yourself as a miracle—someone who came into being through a supernatural encounter with our natural world! It's great to believe that your sperm won. It is even greater when you realize that your sperm had some supernatural help. You are a miracle!

Everybody—You're A Part Of A Family Of Winners

The Olympics must be a really special event to participate in. It must be a wonderful feeling to be one of the greatest athletes in the world and to be competing and living with hundreds of others of the world's best athletes. The Olympics is a great gathering of champions from around the world.

But everyday life itself—in any of the world's metropolises, towns, or villages—is a great gathering of championship human beings. Because the world is full of winners! True, many or even most of them may be thinking and acting like losers, but that doesn't alter the fact. The people you meet day by day are world class people.

We live in a world of winners! Every time you see someone, you see someone whose sperm won the right to his egg!

Gratitude—Appreciate Your Value

Are you ready to say "thank you" yet? Do you appreciate who and what you are? When you appreciate yourself and your blessings you open the door for even greater blessing.

Margaret Storz said: "When we are grateful for the good we already have, we attract more good into our life." Dale Carnegie said: "If you can't have what you want, be grateful for what you have. Keep thinking constantly of all the big things you have to be thankful for instead of complaining about the little things that annoy you." Donald Curtis said: "It is impossible to be negative while we are giving thanks."

Robert Louis Stevenson said: "The person who has stopped being thankful has fallen asleep in life." So say "Thanks!" Stir up within you the attitude of gratitude. As you realize who you are and what you've received, gratitude will flow from you. So don't hold back.

Growth—Go Ahead And Be What You Already Are

You don't have to get to where you already are. If you are playing baseball or softball and are on first base, you don't need to expend time and effort trying to get to first base. Can you imagine a major league player screaming from first base to his team mate at bat, "Come on! Get a hit so I can get to first base!" That is a silly idea.

Maybe you are trying to get to first base in life because you don't realize you are already there! Our society has overrated achievement and underrated realization. If you just realized what you already have, you wouldn't be paying such a high price trying to achieve it. You wouldn't be delaying a personal sense of satisfaction and happiness. Instead you would be enjoying the daily moments of your life.

As Doris Mortman said: "Until you make peace with who you are, you'll never be content with what you have." You are already, right now, in this very moment a great achiever—you are a member of the human race! You are at the pinnacle of success—anything else you accomplish is just the icing on the cake. Believe it! Believe in your present-moment value.

In this book we have been basing your value up to this point on your championship sperm hooking up with your incredible egg. But there is more . . . Turn the page with me to chapter three and see other sources of your value!

"No one else in the wide world since the dawn of time has ever seen the world as you do, or can explain it as you can."
Edith Layton

"Believe that you are capable and worthy of great success."
Greenville Kleiser

Chapter 3

Seven Mighty, Personal Valu-Builders

1) You Have Value To Others

YOU ARE A WINNER because you have or have had value to your family and/or friends. Think about it. How much money would your closest relative or friend take for you? How much would someone have to pay them to never see you, write you, or talk with you again? One dollar? A thousand dollars? A hundred thousand? A million? (I better stop. Someone may take me up on the offer.)

My point is: you are extremely valuable to certain people. How about the reverse of my previous question? How much would your closest relative or friend pay to save your life? One dollar? A thousand dollars? A hundred thousand? All his money and possessions? Give his very life in exchange for yours?

You are extremely valuable because you matter dearly to someone or you have in the past. Maybe you don't feel like it. (Here we go again with those pesky, lying feelings!) Maybe the person who cares so much for you has never fully communicated it to you. Maybe he has acted cold toward you because he was embarrassed to let you know how much he

25

really cares. Maybe he has been hurt and doesn't know how to communicate love. Maybe that person has died.

Here's a fact! If you have ever mattered to even one person, whether you know it or feel it or not, you have had and still have great value! Vi Putnam said: "The entire sum of existence is the magic of being needed by just one person."

2) You Have Value Because Of Your Service

You are a winner because: unless you have lived alone all your life and have never seen or known another human being, you have helped and served somebody. Even babies serve others with their cuteness, sweetness, and innocence. Unless you are a complete hermit, I don't believe you can live without providing some sort of service for somebody.

To serve is to have value. Helen Keller said: "Believe, when you are most unhappy, that there is something for you to do in the world. So long as you can sweeten another's pain, life is not in vain." Martin Luther King, Jr. said: "I just want to help somebody."

If you work, whether you are paid for it or not, you are providing a service. If you cook, clean, and do laundry for someone other than yourself, that's service! If you are running a Fortune 500 company, you are helping somebody. If you wait on customers, you are serving. If you are doing paperwork or computer work, you are helping another human being.

If you are getting a paycheck, you are exchanging value for dollars. But the amount of dollars is not a measure of your value. Someone has said: "Just because you have a lot of money doesn't mean you are worth it."

To help one person one time is of infinite value. While that act of kindness may feel insignificant to you, it is none the less incredibly significant. You don't have to help hundreds or thousands or millions of people to be of value. Hugh Prather said: "It is enough that I am of value to somebody today."

If you are living you are helping–if you are helping you are valuable. If you want to be even more valuable, help a little more. Jesus Christ said: "The greatest among you will be the servant of all."

3) You Have Value Because You Are Alive

Col. WM. C. Hunter said: "The very fact that you are alive is a great thing." You are a winner because you are alive. (I know you are alive or you wouldn't be reading this book.) Just think about how many billions of championship human beings are no longer alive. Their sperm won the right to their egg. They were born, lived, and died. But you, yes you, have something they no longer have–you have life!

Think of all the rich people who are now dead. How about all the famous dead people? There are millions of formerly powerful people who are now dead. You are better off than all of the rich, famous, and powerful dead folks because you still have life.

Solomon said: "There is more hope for a live dog, than for a dead lion." You have great value just because you are alive. Zig Ziglar said: "If you don't think everyday is a good day, just try missing one!" Someone else has said: "Everyday above ground is a good day."

When I hear, think, or read about famous, rich, and powerful dead people, at first I fill a tinge of envy for their accomplishments and/or riches. Then I realize I am better off than they are because I am still alive! Everyday when you wake up, pinch yourself. If it hurts you are still alive! "Still alive"–that's something to celebrate!

When (if) you wake up in the morning you may feel like a loser, but that is a downright lie! Don't believe your lying feelings. Tell yourself the truth–you are a bigger winner than John Kennedy, Cleopatra, Martin Luther King, Jr., Joan of Ark, George and Martha Washington, Solomon, Sojourner Truth, William the Conqueror, Alexander the Great, Elvis Presley, Queen Victoria, Winston Churchill, John Lennon, Janis Joplin, and Lucille Ball; because you are still alive and they are not!

Since you are alive, believe it or not, you have something great and wonderful going for you! Marcus Aurelius said: "When you arise in the morning, think of what a precious privilege it is to be alive–to breathe, to think, to enjoy, to love."

Agatha Christie said: "I like living. I have sometimes been wildly, despairingly, acutely miserable, racked with sorrow, but through it all I still know quite certainly that just to be alive is a grand thing." She believed the truth in spite of her feelings! Follow Agatha Christie's example and choose to experience the value of being alive, even when you don't feel like it!

4) You Have Value Because You Were Created

The works of great artists are of priceless value. According to the United States Declaration of Independence and according to Alcoholics Anonymous you are the work of a great artist and have been created by a Creator! The Declaration of Independence says: "All men are created equal and are endowed by their Creator with certain inalienable rights; that among these are life, liberty and the pursuit of happiness."

Alcoholics Anonymous says: "Deep down in every man, woman and child, is the fundamental idea of God. It may be obscured by calamity, by pomp, by worship of other things, but in some form or other it is there. For faith in a Power greater than ourselves, and miraculous demonstrations of that power in human lives, are facts as old as man himself."

The great psychiatrist, Carl Jung said: "I could not say I believe. I know! I have had the experience of being gripped by something that is stronger than myself, something that people call God."

You didn't crawl out from under a rock. You were created. Your sperm won, but it didn't win alone. You are a miracle because the Creator supernaturally caused your championship sperm to connect with your incredible egg. You beat the impossible odds because you were created. And indeed, that gives you infinite value.

To some people the idea of a Creator is not very appealing. They think it is unscientific to believe in a Creator because you can't prove God in a test tube. You can, however, prove the existence of a Creator in two ways: 1) logic and 2) the laboratory of your life.

1) Logic. If I told you I didn't believe in automobile factories what would you think about me? What if I said I believe that cars just happened? Over millions of years, without any help–without any intelligence–without any manufacturer, cars just showed up on our planet. You would probably think me crazy.

Let me ask you this: Are you not far more complex and complicated than a simple car? If it is crazy to believe that cars just happened, isn't it even more crazy to believe that you just happened? Yes indeed! Logic declares you were created!

2) The laboratory of your life. Listen to your heart. Look at the night sky, the mountains, the sea shore and take note of what you feel inside. Talk to God and observe how it feels. Are you talking to the walls or is there more to it?

Listen to God. Be still and listen to the inner voice. Whose voice do you hear? Are you talking to yourself? Is it imagination? Or is it God? Experiment and explore. Seek. Don't decide on the basis of the theory of evolution or other theories of science. Don't decide on the basis of pain and hurt you've encountered from religion. Don't use your head to explain away invisible reality you encounter. Get beyond your feelings. Don't believe on the basis of tradition or authority. God is real and he can and will show himself to you if you want to know. Don't believe me. Experience for yourself, your value as a created being .

Jim Hartness & Neil Eskelin said: "Just as a store clerk places a new price tag on merchandise, you can examine and attach value to yourself. In doing so, however, don't think about your physical attributes. Think about who created you and the quality of his workmanship." The Creator did an outstanding job when he made you. You have value because you are a masterpiece.

5) You Have Value Because You Are A One-Of-A-Kind

The most valuable things on earth are one-of-a-kind things. If there is only one of it, it is unbelievably costly. Have you noticed that there is only one you?

There has never been anyone like you on this planet before and there never will be again! You are unique! You are one-of-a-kind. You can be identified from every other human being by your fingerprints because no one else has a set like yours.

Your "cheating" feelings want you to believe you are average, common, plain. Nothing can be farther from the truth. You are unique, special, distinctive, rare, uncommon, exceptional, unrivaled, individual, extraordinary, sole (and I don't mean the fish), authentic, peerless, unlike, novel, original, choice, select, matchless, prime, an exclusive, dissimilar, unequaled, unmatched, and unparalleled. You are the one and only you! Now that's value!

Brenda Ueland said: "Since you are like no other being ever created since the beginning of time, you are incomparable."

6) You Have Value Because You Have Ability

You can do things. You have valuable talents and abilities—in fact, you are gifted! You can speak a language. You can read. Read your own resume—you can do a lot of worthwhile things. You even have undiscovered abilities. There are many things you can do that you or no one else knows you can do.

Orison Swett Marden said: "Deep within man dwell those slumbering powers: powers that would astonish him, that he never dreamed of possessing; forces that would revolutionize life if aroused and put into action."

Paul A. Hauck said: "You are a member of the human race, the most spectacular achievement in our world. Though you are imperfect, you are far more gifted than you are faulty." Cecil M. Springer said: "Above all, challenge yourself. You may well surprise yourself at what strengths you have, what you can accomplish."

I once heard a story about a man in the western United States who was shipped one of the first cars ever made. It was a gift from a wealthy friend back east. Having never seen or heard about an automobile before, this man thought it was a carriage, so he hitched up a team of horses and "drove" through town. The townspeople thought his new "carriage" was great.

A few weeks later a stranger came to town and asked, "Why are you pulling your automobile with horses?" The man replied: "What's an automobile?" The stranger helped the man unhitch the horses and showed him how to start the car and drive. The man was amazed to learn the true value of what he actually possessed.

Many human beings, like our friend with the automobile, are completely unaware of what talents and abilities they possess. In this book, I hope to be like that stranger to you. I want to help you start your engine so you can begin to experience the true value of who you are and of the gifts and talents you possess.

Anne Frank said: "Everyone has inside of him a piece of good news. The good news is that you don't know how great you can be. How much you can love! What you can accomplish! And what your potential is!"

I believe that your dreams are obtainable. Your goals are reachable. Your problems are surmountable. Your plans are performable. Your desires are achievable. Your highest aspirations are feasible. Your inner strengths are accessible. Your ideas are workable. And the best life has to offer is within your grasp. All human beings are valuable because they have talents and gifts. But some of them open their packages and some don't! Open up your gifts!

7) You Have Value Because You Are Free

You are not a robot or a puppet on a string. You are not a being controlled by mission control or by any other forces outside yourself. No one has to wind you up in the morning or turn you off at night. No one has to keep you from falling into a ditch or tell you when to eat a meal. No one has to plan your day. You're free.

You have the power to choose. You can be great or you can be small, it is really up to you. Animals run on instincts. You decide what you are going to do. Unlike animals, you can even ignore the instincts that you have, if you choose to do so. As Mencius said: "Those who follow that part of themselves which is great are great, those who follow that part which is little are little." It is your choice.

Even if you feel (not those false feelings again) that your life is worthless and headed for the trash heap, you can choose to change your behaviors, thoughts, and direction. Then you can follow through with a new lifestyle. Now that is value—the value of a fresh start!

You can choose to think better. You can choose to believe better. You can choose to talk better. You can choose to act better. You can choose to be better. And you can choose to persist until you make it happen.

Col. WM. C. Hunter said: "A man by diligent care and practice may absolutely and completely change his whole character, temperament and habits. He may kill undesirable traits of character and replace them with new desirable qualities and faculties. He may eliminate worry and substitute happiness."

Confucius said: "The most intelligent and the most stupid person can in principle change themselves. Only those who ruin themselves, and cast themselves away, and are not willing to learn, are unable to change. In principle, if they are willing to learn, they could change themselves."

The freedom of choice opens the door of your life for greatness. Even if you choose not to follow that part of you which is great; having the ability to choose (should you ever decide to) makes you a person of outstanding value!

Do You See What You Are Worth?

You have just read seven mighty, personal valu-builders! Do you believe them? Do you believe that you are of high value? I hope so. It is important that you know you are valuable. If you think you are worthless, you will act worthless. Like Dr. Kurt Adler said: "Violence is a way of proving one exists when one believes oneself to be insignificant."

If you think you are average, you will act average. But if you think you are valuable, you will act valuable. What do you think about you? It shows in your actions! If you don't believe you are important, read these seven valu-builders daily! Make yourself believe in your value!

Why do you need to value yourself? Odetta said: "The better we feel about ourselves, the fewer times we have to knock somebody else down to feel tall." Iyanla Vanzant said: "When you don't feel good about yourself; it is hard to feel good about anything or anyone else. You see everything with a jaundiced eye. You miss the value and worth of every experience."

Eric Hoffer said: "It is not love of self, but hatred of self which is at the root of the troubles that afflict our world." Sherwood Anderson said: "If a man doesn't delight in himself and the force in him and feel that he and it are wonders, how is all life to become important to him?"

So go for it! Recognize and experience your value! Dr. Harold H. Bloomfield said: "You can experience enormous pleasure in your day-to-day activity if you give yourself permission to appreciate your own magnificence."

William Saroyan said: "Be grateful for yourself. Yes, for yourself. Be thankful. Understand that what a man is he can be grateful for, and ought to be grateful for." Joan Didion said: "To have that sense of one's intrinsic worth which constitutes self-respect is potentially to have everything."

Abraham Lincoln's Advice

World problems are rampant: exploding crime rates, alcohol and drug abuse, gang violence, divorce, stress and burnout, sexual deviancy, teen pregnancy, suicide, short tempers, guns, hatred, dishonesty.

Many people are sounding the alarm that society needs help—more police, gun control, welfare reform, more prisons. Most of the solutions being proposed, however, are attempts to have governments fix society without fixing individual people. But miserable people will continue to make a miserable society no matter what governments do! Until individual human beings become happy and contented, society as a whole will never be peaceful.

Maybe it is time we listen to Abraham Lincoln who said: "It is difficult to make a person miserable while he feels he is worthy of himself and claims kindred to the great God who made him." Lincoln's two keys to avoid personal misery; 1) feeling worthy of yourself (or self-esteem) and 2) claiming kinship to God (or faith), both appear to be in very short supply in our stress-filled society. Could the absence of these two characteristics (self-esteem and faith) be the cause of our current malady?

When someone doesn't value himself what does he do? He does self-destructive behaviors that also cause pain for the people around him. Many behaviors are slowly destructive like self-put-downs, smoking, substance abuse, promiscuity. Other behaviors are rapidly destructive like violent crime.

When someone doesn't believe in God, what does he do? He ignores spiritual values and principles. He lives his life by his own opinions and desires. Thus, we wind up with a smorgasbord culture without a central cohesiveness.

People want governments to fix society. But a society can only be fixed by individuals fixing themselves. Until people value and respect themselves, they won't truly value anything else. Until they acknowledge God they will feel alienated and adrift.

Self-respect comes from self-acceptance, acknowledging that it is alright to be yourself. Most of us have heard so many voices telling us who we are (our parents, peers, teachers, bosses, movies, television, music, advertisements, commercials, aptitude tests) that we don't even know who we are. Many millions live and die as clones, never finding out who they were. The masses feel bound to conform and lose themselves in the sea of society, becoming mindless—living on automatic pilot.

We must break with the voices that attempt to define us as mass produced robots. We must find some stillness and discover who we individually are. We must ask: "Who am I?" "What do I as an individual really want?" "What would I want to do and to be if I didn't care what anybody else thinks about it?" The heartfelt answers to these questions will begin to reveal a self that can be loved and esteemed.

Lincoln's second requirement to avoid misery, faith in God, cannot be manufactured. It only comes from within . . . an inner witness, a still small voice, a gift of revelation. It almost seems insignificant, but its transformational power works for a lifetime. Faith cannot be handed down from parents to children. It must be discovered by each individual. It cannot be produced by ritual or religion, but once found it gives a foundational depth of meaning to life.

There has probably never been a time like today, when so much effort is being expended to produce happiness and so little attention is being paid by individuals to creating the personal qualities that make happiness. Thus misery consumes many of us.

I believe a time will come when we are fed up: when we get tired of blaming what is out there for our misery, and we decide to individually create the personal qualities for happiness—Lincoln's requirements of self-esteem and faith. When that happens for enough people, we will influence society as a whole.

Work daily to build your awareness of your value with these seven mighty, personal valu-builders. And at all costs avoid valu-blockers! What are valu-blockers? Meet me in the next chapter to find out . . .

"It is as necessary to reject untruth as it is to accept truth."
Mahatma Ghandi

"We become enslaved to false notions of what we are and what we ought to be."
Joshua Loth Liebman

Chapter 4

Seven Valu-Blockers

Valu-Blocker 1—Criticism From Other People

IT HURTS TO BE told you are wrong. As Franklin P. Jones said: "Criticism is hard to take, particularly from a relative, a friend, an acquaintance, or a stranger." But don't cringe at criticism. When handled properly, criticism can become an opportunity to improve yourself and your performance.

Since life is full of criticism, we are surrounded by opportunity. Elbert Hubbard said: "To avoid criticism, do nothing, say nothing, be nothing." That is difficult. While successfully handling criticism is not magic, it is much easier than avoiding it altogether. Here are six keys to handling criticism.

1) Decide which type of criticism you are facing. Then you can deal with it effectively. There are four basic types.

A) Concerned criticism. This criticism is based on concern for you as a person. The person giving the critique genuinely cares about your well being and is tactful and gentle. Concerned criticism is helpful, considerate, and usually easy to accept.

B) Constructive criticism. This type of criticism is focused on improving your behavior. It points out what

37

is wrong in order to help you do better. It suggests alternative behaviors and then provides encouragement and support.

C) Casual criticism. Casual or uncaring criticism is difficult to receive. It is often blunt or harsh and is frequently a result of poor judgment. It may be more false than true.

D) Confrontational criticism. This criticism is hostile and may be based on anger, fear, jealousy, or similar negative emotions. It often has an ulterior motive.

2) Concede goodwill or ignorance. Take criticism as friendly. This attitude is for your peace of mind, not your critic's. When you concede goodwill you disarm any negative attitude in the critic and encourage him to become an ally. You might call a person with this goodwill attitude "an inverse paranoid." In reality, everyone is not out to help you, but by holding the belief you may avoid becoming defensive.

What about when the person really is out to get you as in confrontational criticism? In that case concede ignorance! When someone is hostile toward me I like to picture the following scene: I see myself helping an elderly blind man across the street when a bus buzzes by and spooks him. The blind man begins to strike me with his cane. I defend myself and calm him down, but I don't hit him back and I don't get mad. Why? Because he is blind and doesn't understand the situation. The same is true of your hostile critic.

Col. WM. C. Hunter said: "In the morning say to yourself, 'I will not be disturbed by the busybody, the ungrateful, the liar, the deceitful, the envious, the talebearer. They are poor souls who do not know how to control their minds, and I cannot be injured by any one of them.' "

3) Be objective. Look at the facts. Examine the reasons behind the criticism. Is it deserved? Ask yourself: "What is the amount of truth in this criticism?" Ask a friend if he thinks

the criticism is true. If it has little or no truth, then reject it from your mind and life.

Eleanor Roosevelt said: "Living in the public eye accustoms one to accept criticism. One learns gradually to take it objectively and to try to think of it as directed at somebody else and evaluate whether it is just or unjust."

4) Treat factual criticism as an opportunity. It can be a warning, telling you that something in your life needs to be fixed. Solomon said: "He who listens to a life giving rebuke will be at home among the wise. Whoever heeds correction gains understanding." Ask yourself: "What can I do to improve myself based on this criticism?" Devise action steps or goals to help you change.

5) Dismiss untrue criticism. After you have honestly considered the criticism, if it doesn't apply to you, forget about it. Kick it out of your mind. Sophia Loren says: "I like criticism when it is constructive; then it helps me. But when someone is critical just to be mean or tear something down, I must go away from that person."

6) View untrue criticism as a sign of accomplishment. I once heard someone say that the more successful you are, the more you will be criticized. If you are being unjustly criticized a lot, congratulations! You are probably accomplishing something important.

Herbert Hoover said: "We must beware that criticism does not upset our confidence in ourselves." Instead, turn the tables on your critic and let criticism build your confidence. If someone is trying to hold you back, he must be behind you. Col. WM. C. Hunter said: "You know that the greater you are and the stronger you grow, the less you will be disturbed by what the 'they say' mischief maker says about you."

Someone has said: "No one has ever built a statue of a critic." Yet, critics have accomplished a lot in this world. Critics have provided a powerful motivating force for accomplishment. Many successful people have risen to great heights because someone criticized them and told them they couldn't do it! By using these six steps you, too, can turn criticism into a powerful force for positive motivation in your life.

Valu-Blocker 2—Comparing Yourself To Others

As we have already seen, you are a one-of-a-kind. Because you are unique you can't be honestly compared to anyone else on our planet. You might as well compare a peach to the internet, or a vacuum cleaner to a rabbit, or politics to a rock. Do you see? Comparison of radically different things just doesn't make any sense at all. You are so special that you are extremely different from every other human being.

I used to destroy my sense of personal value by comparing myself to others. I thought most people were better looking than me, more confident than me, more popular than me, and I knew for a fact that most people were better athletes than me. I never was (and I'm still not) very good at sports.

Because of the comparisons I was making in my mind, I didn't like myself much. But my comparisons (as yours are) were totally unfair to me. Years ago I read a book by Norman Vincent Peale (I don't remember the title) that helped set me free from my self-imposed dungeon of comparison.

Norman Vincent Peale said that self-comparisons are unfair. He said that everybody is better than you at something. (And I thought "I can't argue with that.") But then he said that you are better than everybody else at something. (And I did argue. "Not me!" I said to myself.)

But as I thought about it I realized that Peale was writing the truth. My feelings said: "You are not better than anybody." But my mind said: "Think about it—it's true—believe the truth." At that point in my life I decided to ignore my feelings of low self-worth, and to believe that I am as valuable as anyone on the planet, regardless of my lying feelings.

From that point in my life I've been working to make my feelings agree with the fact. The fact is that everybody in the world is worse than everybody else at something–and everybody in the world is better than everybody else at something. Whether you feel inferior or superior all depends on what you choose to compare. Therefore comparison is not a valid measure of your value, because you tend to compare your worst traits and abilities to someone else's best traits and abilities. It is not fair to you, so stop it!

St. Bernard (the person, not the dog) said: "I do not want you to compare yourself to those greater or lesser than you, to a particular few, not even to a single person."

Paul of Tarsus said: "We do not dare to classify or compare ourselves with some who commend themselves. When they measure themselves by themselves and compare themselves with themselves, they are not wise." A Hindu proverb says: "There is nothing noble in being superior to some other person. True nobility is being superior to your former self."

I saw a cartoon once that illustrates the futility of comparisons. It showed two cows grazing as a milk truck went by. The truck was painted with a large sign that read: "Homogenized–Pasteurized–Vitamins A & D Added." One cow looked at the other and said: "Makes you feel kind of inadequate, doesn't it?"

As long as you continue to compare yourself to other people you will feel inadequate and you will fail to experience your true value as a human being! So just be yourself. After all, when you are just being yourself, no one can ever tell you that you are doing it wrong!

Valu-Blocker 3—Judging Others/Prejudice

I don't like frog legs! I won't eat frog legs! I find frog legs totally disgusting. But the truth is, I've never given frog legs a chance.

I am so terribly offended with the idea of eating a slimy green wart-maker's legs, that I just can't put those lily pad jumpers in my mouth. (Oh, once or twice I have forced a nibble, but I think my taste buds were petrified. Anyway, I already knew I didn't like it!)

The taste somehow doesn't seem very important to me. Frog legs may taste like: "chicken," "juicy white meat," and other delectable phrases, but I can't taste the chicken for the toad.

I just don't like frog legs! Okay! And I don't like being pressured to give them a sincere try. I don't like them because I don't want to like them!

I guess I might be just a little bit prejudiced. ("A little prejudiced!" you say.) Well, okay. I admit it! When you talk about eating toad toes, I'm jumping to conclusions! I'm like the person who said: "I've got my mind made up, don't confuse me with the facts." Yes, when it comes to eating croaker crutches, I'm the guy who is so narrow minded he can see through a key hole with both eyes at the same time!

Do you see my problem? I'm so offended by frogs (I don't even like tadpoles) that I refuse to give frog meat an honest try. Because of my closed mind, I'm missing the blessing of a delicious (as I am told) food. But I'm willing to pay that price. I'll not change my views merely to tantalize my taste buds.

Besides I can't forget a cartoon I saw years ago. It showed a hospital scene where all the patients were legless frogs on crutches! And yet, I've never seen a protester for frog rights. But then again, I'm not for frog rights. I'm just for my right not to have to be pressured and taunted into eating frog legs! When I want the taste of chicken, I'll eat chicken!

I don't know why I am so prejudiced against frog legs. But if I thought my not eating frog legs was hurting people, I would make myself change. Prejudice is strong, but I could overcome it if I really wanted to.

In the world today, however, there are other, far more dangerous prejudices that need to be avoided and overcome. Hate and racial prejudice appear to be on the upswing. But this upswing in prejudice is about as intelligent as my dislike for frog legs. It is based on feeling rather than fact!

In reality, people are just people. There is not "an us and a them." There is just "a me and a you." And you and I can get along if we get to know each other as individual people. Sure, that takes time and courage and the setting aside of prejudice. But it is worth it, because prejudice hurts people.

The self-respect of some people is trampled by the bigotry of others. In reality the bigot tramples his own self-respect by replacing it with hatred.

Prejudice pervades society. It takes hard work not to automatically classify people according to our cultural stereotypes. I may dislike frog legs (and laugh about it) but I work not to allow myself to fall into prejudice against groups of people.

"Red and yellow, black and white; they are precious in his sight." Anything that obscures that fact is no laughing matter! When you take away from the value of other human beings, you cut off your experience of your own value.

Valu-Blocker 4—Self-Put-Downs

A few years ago I purchased a small, plastic box with six pink buttons, called a "Portable Mom." When you push the buttons a nagging voice says things like: "You're going to put

43

somebody's eye out with that thing." "The answer is no!" "It's broken, are you happy now?"

I use my "Portable Mom" in speeches and seminars to illustrate negative self-talk. After all, everybody has their own, built-in version of a "Portable Mom." We all have inner, negative voices that put us down when our buttons are punched by setbacks and frustrations.

The key to success is to minimize the impact of our inner "Portable Mom" by disputing what it says and by shutting it down as much as possible.

Sometimes "Portable Moms" are hard to shut up! I once spoke for a national association's convention in New Orleans. I took a packed shuttle van from the airport to my downtown hotel. As the van pulled away from the curb I heard a sarcastic voice in the rear of the shuttle say: "It's broken, are you happy now?" My "Portable Mom" was broadcasting negative sentences from my suitcase—non-stop!

I stared forward, hoping that the barrage of negativity would stop. It didn't! I experienced an inner panic attack as my imagination painted vivid images of me and my complaining suitcase being thrown off the bus. I asked myself: "Should I confess when people begin to ask about the disembodied voice showering us all with incessant disapproval?" They didn't. For twenty minutes no one even appeared to notice the put-downs. (Maybe they thought it was their own inner misfortune teller.)

As the van drove away I pondered how we, like the people in the shuttle, often fail to challenge or even question the mental voices that trample our self-esteem. Greenville Kleiser said: "When a thought that is in any way detrimental to your best progress arises in your mind, direct your mind at once to some desirable subject and thus drive out the intruder by substitution."

When left on automatic pilot our minds tend toward negatives. To avoid the turmoil of mental self-deprecation, we must take conscious control of our thinking. Martin Luther said: "A thought is like a bird. You can't stop it from flying across your mind, but you don't have to let it build a nest there."

Three principles for dealing with your inner misfortune teller are: 1) Don't think anything about yourself that you wouldn't allow another person to say to you. 2) Every time you mentally put yourself down, stop and mentally substitute a sincere self-compliment. 3) Frequently repeat the quotation from Paul of Tarsus: "It is a very small thing I should be judged by you or by man's judgment. Yea, I judge not my own self."

Like a hot air balloon, you will soar in the experience of your personal value, when you drop the weights of negative self-talk. Ralph Charell said: "This inner speech, your thoughts, can cause you to be rich or poor, loved or unloved, happy or unhappy, attractive or unattractive, powerful or weak." Blaise Pascal said: "Kind words produce their own image in men's souls; and what a beautiful image it is." Shakespeare summed it up when he said: "Lay aside life-harming heaviness and entertain a cheerful disposition."

Valu-blocker 5—Self-Destructive Behaviors

Someone has said: "If you could kick the person most responsible for your problems, you wouldn't be able to sit down for a week!" Have you ever noticed that human beings do a lot of self-destructive things?

People (myself included) often remind me of the child who goes to her mother or father and says: "Every time I touch it here it hurts." What does the parent usually say? "If it hurts, don't touch it there."

That is simple advice, but profound. If you are doing something that hurts you, stop doing it. Why don't we obey it? Here are twenty false "reasons" why we don't quit self-destructive behaviors and emotions.

1) We use our pride as an excuse for not changing harmful behaviors. It is almost like we think: "If I stop this destructive behavior people will know I was wrong." But we really are not fooling anybody. They know anyway. Most of them are just too kind to mention it to us.

2) We choose to believe our feelings that falsely tell us we can't quit. We forget that we have freedom so we agree to believe a lie.

3) We try to quit and we decide that "It is too hard," or "I'm just not strong enough," or "I'm addicted." So we quit trying.

4) We choose to defend ourselves. So we make dozens of excuses to prove we are right when deep-down, we know we are wrong.

5) We lie to ourselves and deny reality by insisting that the behavior is not really hurting us. We think we are Superman and can't be hurt.

6) We get mad at anyone who tries to help us by suggesting that we change. We tell them to mind their own business and refuse to hear them.

7) We lie and claim that we can quit any time we want to. We tell people we just don't want to.

8) We are unwilling to get professional help. We won't even consider going to a counselor, a psychiatrist, a minister, or even a 12 step group.

9) We tell ourselves and others that we deserve a few faults. Besides they really give us what little pleasure we get out of life, so why should we stop?

10) We preach the falsehood that says: "I'm not hurting anybody but myself. It's my life and it's nobody else's business." We ignore the pain and heartache we are causing all the people who love us.

11) We choose to harden our conscience and refuse to listen to the inner voice that points us away from harmful behaviors.

12) We hurt ourselves so badly with our behaviors that we falsely see our self-destructive behaviors as our only comfort from our pain.

13) We choose to believe that we are not really valuable so we treat ourselves poorly in order to prove that false belief.

14) We want to impress other people and we mistakenly think that if we are as self-destructive as they are, then they will think we are special.

15) We are afraid to be different–to believe in separate values than the people around us–so we self-destruct like they do, just so we will fit in.

16) We were taught a false value system by our parents, schools, television, and we don't want to make the effort to question it.

17) We decide to falsely think that we are too old, or too young, to change.

18) We decide to live on automatic pilot and do the same things we've always done, ignoring the consequences.

19) We are comfortable in our self-destruction and choose to have our familiar misery rather than unfamiliar healing.

20) We have such a low view of ourselves and of humanity that we don't believe living without self-destructive behaviors is possible.

All twenty of these excuses are lies! Put a check mark by each number you agree with. How many of them do you believe?

Your sperm won the right to your incredible egg! You are too good to be stuck in a pack of lies. Don't take it. Don't let your mind be a waste receptacle for the world's dishonesty. A mind is a terrible thing to use as a waste basket! Dump it out. Dump it out. Upgrade the contents of your mind!

Self-destructive behaviors are keeping you from knowing how magnificently valuable you are. Don't stand for it any longer.

Socrates said: "The man with full knowledge would never do evil because the fully enlightened man would recognize the damaging effects on himself."

Value-Blocker 6-Self-Pity

WARNING! WARNING! The next paragraph is exploding with self-pity. If you read it, beware. Don't believe a word of it because it can explode any sense of self-value you have at this moment. Caution. Proceed with care.

"But Steve, you don't understand. I'm pitiful. I really can't change. I'm just a victim. Nobody loves me or even likes me. Nobody cares whether I'm living or dead. I've never had an opportunity. People always ignore me. I can't do any thing right. Even if I tried I couldn't do anything about my life, so why try? This is just my lot in life. It's sad, but hey, I've tried. What's the use in going on? It's all over but the crying. Things will never change. Poor me."

That is self-pity! Elizabeth Elliot said: "Self-pity is a death that has no resurrection, a sinkhole from which no rescuing hand can drag you because you have chosen to sink." It sucks any value you may experience right out of you and leaves you empty. Still, self-pity is very popular. Andre Maurois said: "Self-pity comes so naturally to all of us."

Helen Keller said: "Self-pity is our worst enemy and if we yield to it, we can never do anything wise in this world." Winifred Rhoades said: "To feel sorry for oneself is one of the most disintegrating things the individual can do to himself." Oliver C. Wilson said: "What poison is to food, self-pity is to life." Dede Robertson said: "Self-pity distorts reality and can lead to endless troubles and doubts."

If you are feeling sorry for yourself, go back to chapter one. "Do not pass go. Do not collect $200." Read it again and again. Every time you get a twinge of self-pity think about that championship sperm of yours beating out all those 400 million other fellows. Those 400 million losers are the pitiful ones. Not you. You are a winner!

Valu-Blocker 7-Blame

Let's play the blame game! Not my fault. It's yours. No, it's yours. No, it's yours. No, it's yours. This is going nowhere. Let's find something we can agree on. It's the economy. It's the weather. It's the government. That's a good one. It's congress. It's the president. It's our parents. It's international corporations. It's fur. It's heredity. It's the communists (Oops, they're out of business). It's acid rain. It's talk radio. It's television. It's urbanization. It's poverty. It's affluence. Get the picture?

Blame steals your value because: blame makes you lame. If your feelings and behaviors are somebody else's fault, then you are stuck in concrete. You can't move because you weren't the one responsible for you. You have taken yourself, a championship human being, and essentially put yourself in the position of being valueless.

Let me illustrate. If you say to me: "Steve, why aren't you a better person?" and I say: "It's because I had to go to a bad elementary school," what have I done? I have put myself in a helpless situation.

But if you ask me the same question and I say: "You know, I went to a bad elementary school, but I chose to make the best of it," I've turned it around. By accepting responsibility I have removed myself from the position of victim and put myself in a position of value and of power.

Earl Nightingale used to tell the story of two brothers. When these two brothers were small children their father robbed a store and killed the clerk. He was convicted and sent to prison. When these two brothers were in their thirties, one of them had a good job, a nice family, and was a productive citizen. The other one was in prison. He had robbed a store.

Both of the brothers were asked the same question. "How did your life turn out the way it did?" Remarkably, they gave the same answer: "How could I have done anything else with a father like I had?"

One brother used his tragedy to blame, to become lame, and to feel valueless. The other brother used it as an example of what not to do and took responsibility on himself to make something valuable of his life.

Are you blocking your value with blame, or receiving your value with responsibility?

Bust Up The Valu-Blockers

Mother Teresa said: "The biggest disease of today is not leprosy or tuberculosis, but rather the feeling of being unwanted." Billions of people allow their vision of their value to be blocked. They feel unwanted, unloved, valueless. But there is great hope. The truth can still be heard.

Come on to the next chapter and meet two people: Charlie, a valu-blinder, and Mary, a valu-finder.

"It is wisest and best to fix our attention on the beautiful and the good, and dwell as little as possible on the evil and false."
Robert Cecil

"You must get in helpful thoughts and shut out hurtful thoughts. Helpful thoughts bring strength; hurtful thoughts cause weakness."
Col.WM. C. Hunter

Chapter 5

Valu-Blinders And Valu-Finders (Charlie and Mary)

Magic Coloring Book Illustrates The Valu-Blinder

I HAVE A MAGIC coloring book. I know it is magic because it says "magic" right on the cover. I use my magic coloring book in my speeches and seminars to illustrate three kinds of people.

When I flip through my coloring book the first time, every page has ugly marks and X's on it. I use this to illustrate the valu-blinder. A valu-blinder finds ugliness and negatives on every page of his life. He thinks he is a loser because he is blind to his value. He acts like his sperm lost the race, but of course, if that was the case he wouldn't be here to grumble. The valu-blinder gets a $10,000 raise and what does he say? "This is terrible...I've got to pay income tax on this!"

Charlie's Story

A valu-blinder is someone with a nice, even disposition-miserable all the time! A few years ago I met a classic valu-blinder. I went to work for a real estate firm and on my first day the gentleman in the next cubicle introduced himself to me. He stuck out his hand and said: "Hi. I'm Charlie. You're not going to like working here!"

I shook his hand and said: "I'm Steve. How do you know?"

He said: "Because nobody likes working here!"

I asked: "Then why are you working here?"

Charlie said: "Well I've got to have a job and this is better than nothing. Although not much. Besides, I can retire in a couple of years."

I worked close to Charlie for a year or so. Every morning Charlie would get a cup of coffee and I would hear him grumbling next to me: "This coffee is too hot!" Ten minutes later Charlie would be mumbling with various expletives: "My coffee is too cold!" I never once heard Charlie say: "My coffee is just right."

Let me ask you a question. How did Charlie's coffee get from too hot to too cold without passing by just right? Is that possible? Can coffee suddenly drop ten degrees? I don't think so. Let me ask you this. Was the problem with the coffee or was the problem with Charlie? You are right indeed, Charlie was a dedicated valu-blinder. Just like my magic coloring book, every page of his life was filled with ugliness.

(By the way, being a valu-blinder is not always bad. If you ever have to borrow money, borrow it from a valu-blinder because she doesn't think you are going to pay her back anyway!)

Magic Coloring Book Illustrates
The-Bland-Leading-The-Bland

In speeches, after I tell the Charlie story, I pick up my magic coloring book and flip through it again. This time every page has an uncolored picture on it. I tell my audience that this represents the second group of people—the-bland-leading -the-bland. This is the mediocre group—not too negative, but not very positive either.

When you ask a BLB how he is doing, he says "fine." What is fine? Fine is average—not good, not bad. Being a BLB is better than being a valu-blinder, but it still leaves a lot to be desired. I won't give you an example of a BLB because the world is full of BLB's—world championship human beings who are walking around the planet, thinking and acting like lackluster people.

Magic Coloring Book Illustrates The Valu-Finder

After I talk about the-bland-leading-the bland (BLB) I pick my magic coloring book up a third time and flip through it. This time every page contains a beautiful, full-color picture. This represents the valu-finder.

A valu-finder is someone who sincerely recognizes and appreciates his value. No matter what happens in his life a valu-finder sees something good in it. But a valu-finder is not into denial.

A false definition of a valu-finder would be: a valu-finder is a man who comes home from work at night and finds cigar butts scattered all over his house—he then sits back in his recliner and says: "I see, my wife has quit smoking cigarettes." That is not being a valu-finder. Denial would probably be a better name for it. The gentleman should at least ask his wife: "Honey, did you have some company today?"

A true definition of a valu-finder is: a valu-finder is a person who gets treed by a bear and then sits back and enjoys the view. Oh yes, he avoids denial and faces reality. He might say, "If that bear doesn't stop shaking this tree, I may end up being his lunch." But he doesn't get stuck in partial reality. He also admits to the reality that he is safe so far. He may say: "Well, he hasn't eaten me yet and it is a wonderful day. Look

53

at the beautiful view from here." A valu-finder can enjoy life's scenery, even on a detour.

Mary's Story

A few years ago I met a classic valu-finder. Her name was Mary. Her brother was a friend of mine. He told me that Mary was in the hospital, dying from cancer and according to her doctors, only had two weeks to live. Then he asked me to go see her.

I felt (those deceptive feelings again) very un-comfortable about dealing with Mary's situation and since I didn't know her I stalled for two weeks. But her brother told me that Mary was still alive and once again asked me to go see her. I figured I couldn't get out of it this time.

As I entered Mary's room I introduced myself and told her that her brother had asked me to come and see her. "Did he tell you what's wrong with me?" she asked.

I told her that he had told me all about her. And she replied that it was true she had cancer and the doctors thought she would have died by then. Then Mary totally surprised me. She said: "But I'm not going to let that ruin my day. I'm alive today and I'm going to make the very best of the day."

We had a delightful conversation. During the next thirty minutes she never mentioned the cancer again. She told me what a beautiful view she had from her window. She made it sound so good I had to stand up and look out. All I saw were ugly hospital roof tops. But Mary saw birds, blue sky, "beautiful white clouds."

Mary told me how good the hospital food was. (That's when I thought that maybe she was in denial.) When I left Mary's room I felt like doing the Wrigley's Spearmint Gum thing. Toyota does it too—that thing where someone jumps up and clicks his heels together. But I'm too uncoordinated. Besides, the nursing station was just outside her door and a couple of nurses were watching me. (At that moment, I believed one of the lies of our society and didn't want the nurses to see me being too happy—but how can anyone possibly be too happy?) I walked over and asked the nurses about Mary. "Is she on drugs?" I inquired.

"Yes she is," a nurse replied.

"That explains why she is in such a good mood," I said.

"You don't understand," the nurse told me. "The drugs are not influencing her thinking. She really is that positive."

I was amazed. On my way home I thought about Mary and I decided to go visit her again and see if I could learn her secret. Of course I had to hurry because she didn't have much time left, so during the next week I went to see her three or four times.

I remember the last time I went into her room. She looked rather somber and said: "Last night I saw Jesus Christ standing at the foot of my bed and he told me that he is taking me home today."

"Oh no!" I said, thinking she meant he was taking her to Heaven.

Mary smiled and said: "No, you don't understand. The doctor came in this morning and confirmed it. I'm in remission and I'm going home to my house."

And Mary did go home. She lived two more years and I got to know her better. Mary's life had not been all peaches and cream, but somehow she had learned to find the good. Like my magic coloring book, every page of her life was filled with color and beauty.

I Can Sit Up And Take Nourishment

A friend of mine, Jerry, once told me about an experience he had with a valu-finder. He got on the elevator in a hospital and as the door closed, Jerry noticed he was alone on the elevator with an elderly man. Jerry said the fellow looked emaciated, like a POW. He was slumped over in a wheelchair, about to fall out and had an IV in his arm. To Jerry, the man was so thin and frail that he looked like he was about to die.

Jerry told me that as the door closed the old man began to hum a cheerful tune. Jerry said to him: "Good morning, Sir."

The fellow answered by saying: "Good morning to you, too, Sonny!"

Jerry responded: "You must be doing all right today."

The old man said: "You bet, Sonny! I can sit up and take nourishment!" It just doesn't take much for a true valu-finder to discover value and appreciation in life.

The Answer To Life—
It's All In Where You Put Your Thumb

I used to think that valu-finders were magical...that they lived charmed lives...that everything always turned out great for them. But Mary convinced me that just isn't so. I think Charlie had the easier life, but Mary was the one who experienced and delighted in her value.

How about the coloring book, is it magic? In my speeches and seminars I always ask the audience if anyone knows how my coloring book works. Usually a few people have paid close enough attention to have discovered the secret and they yell out: "You are moving your thumb!"

"That's it!" I say. "You have discovered the secret to a successful and happy life. It's all in where you put your thumb!" People usually laugh. But that is not a joke. It is the absolute truth. The victorious secret to whether you are happy or sad, a valu-finder or a valu-blinder, a success or a failure—is all in where you put your mental thumb!

Let me explain. The pages of the coloring book are specially cut so that if you put your thumb at the bottom and flip through the book you get all the pages with ugly marks on them. If you put your thumb at the top and flip you get all the pages that are uncolored. And if you put your thumb at the middle and flip you get all the beautiful, full-color pages.

You Are Like My Magic Coloring Book

Your mind is exactly like the coloring book. If you put your mental thumb in a certain place you will get all the ugly pages of your life. If you put your mental thumb in another place you can get all your mediocre pages. But if you put your mental thumb in another place you will get all the beautiful pages of your life.

Everybody is like the coloring book. We all have plenty of ugly pages in our lives. We all have scads of average pages. And we all have a good deal of wonderful pages. Charlie, Mary, you, and me. Our lives are basically the same—full of bad, good, and so-so. The difference between us is not our circumstances, but where we put our mental thumb.

A valu-finder is not someone who is born with a positive disposition. That would rule me out. I am basically a pessimist, just ask my wife, Ernie. I have to work very hard on myself to experience my value. It is not easy, but it is sure worth it (just ask Ernie). The good news for you is if I can do it, so can you.

So What's The Real Difference?

A valu-blinder forgets to laugh at his problems, while a valu-finder laughs to forget his problems. A valu-finder looks at an oyster and expects to find a pearl, while a valu-blinder looks at an oyster and expects to get ptomaine poisoning.

A valu-blinder prefers familiar trouble rather than an unfamiliar solution. He enjoys stewing without doing. A valu-blinder doesn't believe in anything and wants everybody else to share his belief with him. A valu-blinder awfulbatizes his life.

A valu-blinder often winds up wanting what he fears, so he can prove that he was right in fearing it in the first place. A valu-blinder has his eyes glued on the negative, while a valu-finder is encouraged by the positive.

A valu-blinder looks for sympathy, a valu-finder spreads good cheer. A valu-blinder complains, while a valu-finder obtains. Difficulty causes the valu-blinder to break, but it causes the valu-finder to break records.

A valu-finder expects his dreams to come true, while a valu-blinder expects his nightmares. A valu-finder counts his blessings, while a valu-blinder tallies his troubles. A valu-finder hears opportunity knock, while a valu-blinder knocks opportunity. A valu-finder is wrong just about as often as a valu-blinder, but he sure has more fun! A valu-finder thinks the fly buzzing around the window just wants out of the house.

A person has two ends—a sitting end and a thinking end. Where the thinking end goes, the sitting end follows. So if you don't like where you find your bottom, change what you're thinking at your top. Whether you are a valu-finder or a valu-blinder, depends to a large degree on which end you choose to use—heads you win, tails you lose!

Samuel Smiles summed it up when he said: "We may make the best of life or we may make the worst of it, and it depends very much upon ourselves whether we extract joy or misery from it."

In the rest of this book we are going to look at some practical ways you can move your mental thumb from valu-blinding to valu-finding—powerful techniques.

As for now, however, follow me into the next chapter and learn to be a bouncer.

.

"It is never too late to be what you might have been."
George Eliot

"Troubles are usually the brooms and shovels that smooth the road to a good man's fortune."
St. Basil

Chapter 6

Be A Bouncer--Not A Splatterer

Here's To Bouncers!

HERE'S TO BOUNCERS! In my opinion bouncers are the most successful people on earth—bar none! They have learned the art of how to handle themselves. And bouncers know the victorious secret of life: It's not how far you fall, it's how well you bounce when you hit bottom!

As we have seen there are three types of people: valu-finders, BLBs, and valu-blinders. Bouncers are valu-finders. Splatterers are valu-blinders. When splatterers hit rock bottom in life they fall apart and stick to the bottom like glue! (And they make a major mess doing it.)

Bouncers, however, spring back. True, sometimes it takes them awhile, but sooner or later, the very obstacle they collided with propels them back toward the top.

How can you be a bouncer? Motivational speaker, Les Brown, says: "If you can't fight or you can't flee, flow!"

Bouncers are flexible. They know how to change, flow, bend, and grow! Bouncers are mentally tough. They control their attitudes, thoughts, and emotions.

Bouncers make the very best of whatever hand they are dealt. They agree with Clarence Goshorn who said: "If I would venture a forecast, I would say that business will be good this year for those who make it good."

Bouncers blast past the past. They refuse to play the place-the-blame-game. Bouncers have inner strength. They believe in themselves and they turn a deaf ear to lying feelings.

Bouncers see their difficulties as opportunities for self-development. Anybody can gain from their successes, but bouncers know how to profit even from their losses.

Bouncers may from time to time tire out, but they never completely quit or give up on themselves. Bouncers know that whatever is bigger than they are gives them the opportunity to be bigger than they have been.

Bouncers are optimists. They agree with Winston Churchill who said: "I am an optimist. It doesn't seem too much use being anything else."

Here's to bouncers, valu-finders, optimists! Hip hip hurrah!

A Real-Life Bouncer From The Sixteenth Century

Lorenzo Scupoli, a Sixteenth Century Italian monk said: "If you are active in setting up good thoughts and dispositions in yourself morning, evening and at all other hours of the day, invisible foes will never come near you."

Many people believe the positive thinking and self-help movement is a development of Twentieth Century America. Much credit is correctly given to Norman Vincent Peale, Dale Carnegie, and Napoleon Hill as pioneers of the modern self-help movement. Yet throughout history some people have believed and taught the power of positive thinking.

Take Lorenzo for example. He said: "Preserving peace of heart should be the constant endeavor of your whole life." It wasn't easy for Lorenzo. In 1585 he was accused of a "scandalous offense." History is not clear about the nature of the charge or who the accuser was. What is clear, however, is that Lorenzo was removed from the priesthood and sentenced to a long and severe penance. He suffered severe public disgrace for fourteen years, until his complete innocence was finally acknowledged around 1599.

In the midst of his trials Lorenzo Scupoli wrote a book called *Spiritual Combat*. It was first published in 1589, about four years after his being falsely condemned. Remarkably the book contains no bitterness. Instead it is full of positive thinking techniques which he calls "inner actions."

Lorenzo says, most probably thinking about his own painful experience: "When the heart is thrown into turmoil, everything within us is brought into disorderly movement and our very mind loses the capacity of right thinking. This is why it is so necessary not to delay in quietening the heart as soon as it becomes troubled by something internal or external."

Knowing the hard work of overcoming negative thoughts he says: "Your constant care should be not to let your heart become agitated or troubled, but to use every effort to keep it peaceful and calm."

Lorenzo also practiced what today we call "time management." He said: "The time you have in your hands is priceless and if you waste it uselessly, the hour will come when you will seek and not find it."

To develop gratitude Lorenzo suggests: "Examine all God's favors to mankind and to you, yourself; and go over them frequently in your thought, rehearsing them in your memory."

Do people in our day have it any harder than Lorenzo Scupoli did? Maybe you have suffered unjustly. Maybe you have been mistreated. Maybe the daily grind has made you weary. Maybe you're discouraged or just mentally tired.

Lorenzo said: "Peace of heart is the aim...As soon as the heart is quieted, the struggle is over."

If Lorenzo Scupoli could bounce back from his troubles, so can you! Make yourself think positive. Work hard on yourself. Use your time well. Be grateful. Be a Twenty-First century bouncer! But how?

Eight Ways To Bounce Back

So how do bouncers do it? How exactly do they "never give up?" How is it that they "try and try again?" Is it sheer will power, stubbornness, natural grit, discipline...?

The answer seems to be all of the above and more. Bouncers repel discouragement by embracing the following eight "go-again" attitudes:

1) Bouncers View Failure Favorably.

Robert Allen said: "There is no failure, only feedback." Failure is successfully discovering something that doesn't work. It is a learning experience.

Bouncers see in failure the hope and encouragement of a stepping stone. This gives them the desire to get up and go again. Splatterers see in failure the finality of a tombstone. This causes them to lose heart and quit.

2) Bouncers Keep Their Expectations Realistic.

A mountain climber doesn't leave base camp and begin his ascent toward the summit of Mt. Everest only to quit after 25 steps. He keeps things in proper perspective. He knows that reaching his goal will require many thousands of steps and maybe even hundreds of slips.

Bouncers know that reaching their goals will require time and effort and setbacks. They don't expect to reach their summit overnight. They are mentally prepared to strive for the long haul. They expect to fall and get up many times along their journey to the top.

3) Bouncers Vary Their Approaches.

Brian Tracy in the tape series, "The Psychology of Achievement," tells about four men who became millionaires by the age of 35. Each one was involved in an average of 17 businesses before he found the business that made him rich. Splatterers usually make the same attempts over and over again until they become discouraged and quit.

Bouncers, however, make many different attempts at success. If one thing doesn't work, they are not easily discouraged, yet they do not blindly repeat the same thing. Instead, they get up and go again from another angle. They try something different.

4) Bouncers Create Or Embrace A "Have-To."

Famous military leaders have inspired their troops to great accomplishment by burning their boats or bridges. Necessity really is the mother of achievement. People who have to, find a way. But when getting up is an option, it is very easy to splatter instead of bounce.

Dick Garner said: "By and large you will do what you have to do; not much more and not much less." He suggested letting your needs create a "have-to."

5) Bouncers Find And Develop A Goal That Pulls.

A goal without a burning desire is like kissing your sister or brother. You'll do it when you have to, but you probably wouldn't knock yourself out for the privilege.

How can you create desire? The New Testament says: "Where your treasure is, there will be your heart also." Invest your treasure of time in your goal. Think about it. Write it down in detail. Visualize yourself enjoying the rewards of your goal. Hang up pictures of it. Talk about it. Soon your heart will crave it. And the next time you fall along the way, your desire will cause you to jump up and go again.

6) Bouncers Reject Rejection.

People who try again and again do not base their self-worth on their performance. They have an internally based self-image. They do not tell themselves: "I am a failure."

Instead they say: "That didn't work out, but I am still a winner." And when they have fallen down and are on the ground, they know that being down is not their home. They know that they came from a championship sperm and an incredible egg, so they get up and go again.

7) Bouncers Enjoy And Value The Effort.

They see work as its own reward. Everybody enjoys pay checks or other payoffs, but a persister enjoys the experience and the challenge of what he does. As someone has said: "If money is your only reward for your work, then you are vastly underpaid, no matter how much money you make."

8) Bouncers Budget Their Effort.

Some people wear themselves out and have no energy left for life. But those who continually get up and go again have found a way to balance their effort. As Kenny Rogers sang, "They know when to hold 'em and know when to fold 'em." Bouncers know when to take a break and they know when to try again. They are willing to rest and to sharpen their skills when they need to.

These eight "go again" attitudes are not spontaneous. They are not standard equipment for human beings. They must be diligently cultivated and developed. They must be incessantly kneaded into your thoughts. Only then will they empower you to get up and go again!

Bouncers Are In For The Long Haul

How far can you go on one step? Only three or four feet from where you are! No significant distance at all! Even the world's best long jumpers can only jump twenty something feet in one step. The bottom line is one step goes nowhere. It accomplishes nothing. Zilch.

Does that mean walking is not a valid method of transportation? Hardly! How far can you go on five million one hundred thousand steps? From the Empire State Building to the Hollywood Bowl!

How much can you improve your life or your career with one uplifting thought? None. Nada. Zilch. One positive thought does nothing! Because of that fact, many people have falsely concluded that positive thinking is not a valid method of building a successful life and career.

One positive thought is worthless. But how much can you improve your life with five million one hundred thousand uplifting thoughts? Say hello to Hollywood and your starring role of success in life! With that many positive thoughts you can indeed achieve greatness at work and in life! Only five million ninety-nine thousand nine hundred and ninety-nine uplifting thoughts to go!

Genuine success requires positive thinking over time. Like one tiny tile in a huge mosaic, one moment in time or one event in your life (whether positive or negative) is impotent. Life seldom works by instant transformation. Today I'm almost always exactly the same as I was yesterday. But if I make a tiny self-improvement in my thinking every day, in a decade I'll be remarkably different than I am today. One step at a time!

You can get there from where you are—wherever you want to go! Not all at once like they do on *Star Trek*. No one is going to "beam you up" and put you where you want to be. Not luck. Not more money. Not a new spouse. Not getting rid of an old spouse. Not a promotion. Not even your dream job will "beam you up" to where you want to be.

But you can get there from where you are. Your career will follow your brain. When you get your mind and emotions where you want them to be (one step at a time) your circumstances will follow.

Samuel Smiles, author of the book *Self-Help* which was published more than a hundred years ago, said: "Fifteen minutes a day spent on self-improvement will be felt at the end of a year!" Tony Robbins says: "You can do far less than you think you can in a year, but you can do far more than you think you can in a decade!"

Where are you on the road of five million one hundred thousand positive thoughts to outstanding success in life? Samuel Smiles also said: "Great results cannot be achieved at once; and we must be satisfied to advance in life as we walk, step by step."

Take the next step by going into chapter 7 and learning "How To Experience Positive Change In Your Feelings."

"I don't wait for moods. You accomplish nothing if you do that. Your mind must know it has got to get down to work."

Pearl Buck

"Your whole circle of friends, your home and everything with which you come in contact changes aspect with every change in your mood or view."

Col. WM. C. Hunter

Chapter 7

How To Experience Positive Change In Your Feelings

Experiencing Your Value Is Not Automatic

YOU'VE NOW BEEN through six chapters—you have read hundreds of statements that illustrate and prove your value as a human being. But you still may not have the experience of feeling valuable. That is our goal in this book—that you experience the joy and peace of feeling valuable.

We have already seen how your feelings may be false. All of us are constantly attacked by throngs of lying feelings and thoughts. We feel and think many things that are absolutely untrue. The first six chapters of this book have been my attempt to show you the truth—the truth that you, yes you, are infinitely valuable.

Have I written anything so far in this book that is untrue about you? Disprove me if you can. Attempt to argue against what I have written. Intellectually prove that you are worthless, if you so please. I have no problem with that.

But don't write me off because you don't yet feel valuable. Because you will never—no never—feel valuable until you first believe you are valuable. Paul of Tarsus wrote: "We are led by faith (belief) not by sight (experience or feelings)." As human beings we are designed to be led by our inner beliefs, not by our feelings. Someone has said: "The test of courage is not to give up but to rise up and take dominion over melancholy moods!"

An Experiment For You To Do

Our ability of self-control is at the level of intellectual belief, not at the level of feelings. You and I have almost no direct control over our feelings. Try an experiment with me. Think about someone you dislike. Visualize that person in your mind for a few seconds, until you begin to feel negative feelings about him or her. Now turn those negative feelings about that person into positive feelings and make yourself feel love for that person.

Can't do it, can you? Let's try something else. Think about a food you find revolting. Visualize that food in your mind for a few seconds. Remember what it tastes like until you begin to feel negative feelings about it. Now turn those negative feelings about that food into positive feelings and make yourself feel eager to eat that food.

Can't do that either, can you? At the level of feelings you have very little ability to control yourself. But you, yes you, are more than your feelings—you are also your intellectual beliefs and thoughts. And you do have the power to change on that level!

Back To Our Experiment

Let's go back to our experiment. Once again, think about the person you dislike. Visualize him in your mind. Feel those negative feelings again. Now while you are feeling the negative feelings choose to think a kind thought about the person. For example, make your mind think: "I hope he has a good day." Can you think that thought about the person you dislike? Of course you can think that! You may not feel it. You may not really mean it. But you can think it!

This experiment proves that you, yes you, do have the ability to control your thoughts. You can feel bad things about somebody and yet think good things. What about the food? Once again, think about the food you find revolting. Visualize it in your mind. Remember how revolting it tastes to you. Now while you are feeling negative feelings about the food, choose to think something good about it. For example, make your mind think: "If I was starving, this revolting food could keep me alive."

Can you think that thought about the food you find revolting? I don't mean can you feel it, but can you think it? Of course you can. I hate frog legs as you have already seen in this book. But I can think good thoughts about frog legs, even though it makes me shudder when I do. I still have power over my thoughts and so do you!

It's A Proven Fact –
You Absolutely Can Choose Your Thoughts

If you did the experiment with me you have proven that you, yes you, are indeed able to control your thoughts. If you haven't done the experiment, why haven't you? Do you not want to know the truth about yourself? You are not the victim that you may think you are! Go ahead, do the experiment and discover your power to choose thoughts.

James Allen said: "He who would be useful, strong, and happy must cease to be a passive receptacle for the negative, beggarly, and impure streams of thought; and as a wise householder commands his servants and invites his guest, so must he learn to command his desires and to say, with authority, what thoughts he shall admit into the mansion of his soul."

So What's The Big Deal About This Experiment?

Some of you may be thinking, "So what? I can choose to think good thoughts about people and food I don't like. So what's the big deal?"

Here's the deal: if you can change your thoughts, you can eventually change your beliefs—and when your beliefs change your feelings will automatically change.

When I was in the fourth grade, my family moved from Little Rock, Arkansas, to Jonesboro, Arkansas. I had donuts for breakfast, before I went to my last day at my old school. At mid-morning I vomited in class. The teacher attempted to console me and cleaned up my mess.

I felt unconsoled. I felt sick. I felt humiliated. And I felt like donuts were the worst food in the world! I believed that the donuts gave me all these bad feelings. From that day on, I didn't like donuts. When I saw other people enjoying donuts, to me it looked like an insane act. How disgusting!

For years, every time I saw or heard about donuts, I thought to myself how disgusting they were and I felt disgusted.

But as time went on I began to notice that very few people who ate donuts vomited later that day. And I thought about that observation. Maybe the donuts were not the reason I vomited in the fourth grade. Still, I felt like donuts were awful so I continued to avoid them. But donuts are every-where (they are much more common than frog legs). I mean, it seems like almost everybody eats donuts. For years, every time I saw a donut I would feel repulsed, but then I would think (yes, think): "Donuts must not be that bad because everybody but me eats them."

In my early twenties, after years of feeling bad about donuts, but thinking that maybe my feelings were wrong, somebody offered me a donut hole—just a little tiny hole. At that point I couldn't see any great harm in a donut hole, so I bit off a nibble—and wonder of wonders—I liked it! As my taste buds savored the flavor, my feelings danced in delight. Then I got really brave and tried a chocolate-covered, cream-filled model, and it was wonderful!

Would you believe that I eat donuts now? Would you believe that when I see a donut shop I feel good instead of bad? What happened to me? Three things!

Three Steps To Changing Your Feelings

1) I changed my thoughts and made them disagree with my feelings. It is not comfortable to disagree with your own feelings. My feelings hated donuts but I made my thoughts think that donuts couldn't be as bad as I felt about them.

This is the stage where most people give up. They think their feelings are true. As we have seen, however, feelings are much more likely to be false than systematic, rational thought.

2) I continued to think about donuts contrary to my feelings for several years. (Remember one step or one thought won't take you very far.) Over time my inward belief about donuts began to conform to my thoughts and my logic, rather than to my feelings.

In other words, repeating my new thought over time got the truth about donuts from my head to my heart. (More on this in a moment.)

3) I developed a new belief about donuts and the new belief caused me to feel differently about donuts. When I believed donuts to be horrid I hated them, but when I began to believe that they were probably all right, I began to feel

completely different. Instead of feeling like vomiting at the sight of a donut, I began to feel like trying one. So I finally did. And after one bite I was hooked on donuts. Aren't they wonderful?

From The Head To The Heart

We have seen that you can have direct control over your thoughts if you choose to do so. We have also seen that you can have very little direct control over your feelings, no matter how hard you try. Thoughts occur in your mind. Feelings occur in your heart.

Many times as human beings, we know something in our mind, but we don't feel it in our heart. We may know in our head that it is Christmas time and "'tis the season to be jolly," but we may feel in our heart like Mr. Scrooge.

We may know in our head that we are lucky to be alive, but we may feel in our heart that we don't know how much more we can take. In your head you may agree with the truths I have presented about your personal value, but in your heart you may feel worthless. There is a gap between your head and your heart!

The Gap—Between Your Head And Your Heart

If I was to tell you that every twenty seconds in America an automobile is stolen, you would have a bland fact in your head. We call that information. But if someone ran up to you while you were reading this and yelled: "Excuse me for interrupting your book, but your car has just been stolen!" you would have a powerful feeling in your heart! We call that inspiration!

Is the truth we have demonstrated about your personal value a bland fact in your head? Or is it a powerful feeling in your heart?

Most of us have a gap between what we know (our facts) and our emotions (our beliefs producing our feelings). That gap is the Gulf Against Perception. To bridge the GAP we have to move beyond thoughts to belief. We must transform our thinking into believing.

But how can we turn our bland information into dynamic inspiration? How do we get from "know-about" to "believe-like?"

One way is to use an ARC. The dictionary defines an arc as: "the band of sparks between two closely placed electrodes when a current leaps the gap from one to another." We've all experienced moments when our minds have been sparked to leap from dry facts to a strong belief, when an arc jumps our mental GAP (Gulf Against Perception). Such moments raise us to new levels of belief in a quantum leap of inspiration.

How do we ARC the Gulf Against Perception? There are three keys represented by ARC. They are Affirmation, Repetition, and Contagion.

1) Affirmation: An affirmation is a present tense, positive statement about who you are and what you can do. Examples are: "I am an extremely valuable person!" "I am always confident." "I believe in myself and in my ability to make a difference in the world!"

2) Repetition: Repetition recognizes that a one-time statement or thought has little impact on our lives. In 1908 Gustave LeBon, in the book, *The Crowd*, said: "The repeated statement is embedded in the long run in those profound regions of our unconscious selves in which the motives of our actions are formed."

To bridge the Gulf Against Perception we must make tens of thousands of repetitions of our affirmations. A practical way to do this is to repeat affirmations in your mind through-out the day and when you are lying in bed prior to sleep. Counting repetitions helps you to keep your focus.

3) Contagion: Contagion is the point when we "catch" the truth of our affirmation. Gustave LeBon said: "At the end of a certain time we have forgotten who is the author of the repeated assertion, and we finish it by believing it."

That is the moment when the ARC bridges the GAP between knowledge and emotion—between information and inspiration! When you really believe your affirmation you will live it. Gustave LeBon said: "To endow a man with faith is to multiply his strength tenfold."

Do you want to change your beliefs so that they conform to the truth about you and your world? Use the ARC – Affirmation (Say it), Repetition (Continue saying it), Contagion (Catch it).

In the long run (5-10 years) the daily, habitual practice of ARC will produce amazing results in your life!

Think The Truth—Speak The Truth!

So choose to think the truth, not your feelings. Jawaharla Nehru said: "Most people unfortunately do not think. They feel and act according to their feelings." Think the truth over and over and over and over again. You can do it. Think truth about you, not lies! "Your sperm won and you are a champion!" Think it, think it, I said THINK IT!

And go a step further-say it! Speak the truth about yourself, not the lies. Don't whine and say a bunch of false nonsense, like "I can't do anything right," or "Nobody loves me." Kill those value-stealing lies! When you catch yourself speaking a lie, take it back. Say out-loud: "I didn't mean that— it is not true about me! I am a winner—that is the truth." (You don't have to bring a sperm or an egg into the conversation if you don't want to.)

Speak truth about you! Don't wait for your feelings to give you permission. Speak the truth anyway! Speak it! SPEAK IT! I say it again: SPEAK IT!

If I could be more emphatic, I would. If I could grab your face and move your lips and make you say the truth about how amazingly valuable you are, I would! But I can't! If it is to be, it is up to you-know-who (that means you)! It is up to you to move your own mind and to move your own lips according to the truth about you rather than letting lying feelings push you around. Do it! Just do it!

An Ernie & Steve Example

Not too long after I married my wife, Ernie, (yes, she is female) she said something really negative about herself. I remember her saying something like: "I'm such an idiot." (She thinks she said something else, but she is not sure what.)

Before I knew it I found myself saying: "Stop it!"

"What do you mean?" Ernie said.

"I don't want anyone calling my wife an idiot (we'll go with my memory here), not even my wife!" I said.

"I never thought about that," Ernie replied.

Have you ever thought about the fact that if you call yourself an idiot (or any other negative name for that matter) you are putting down someone that your family and your best friends love very much? How would you like someone to put down your mother or father, son or daughter, brother or sister, husband or wife, friend or companion? You would probably get mad and tell the person (very emphatically) to stop it.

We'll put the shoe on the other foot. If you don't want anybody putting down the people you care about, then you stop putting down yourself.

I had been using this example in speeches for three years, when I asked a guy to help me with a very public project. I didn't know him very well so I thought I should check with some people who knew him. I got a pretty bad report on him and told Ernie about it. We decided that the only thing I could do was to ask him to step down from the project.

So about two hours after I asked for his help, I found myself telling him that I couldn't use him after all. He was obviously hurt and offended. I felt terrible. For the next week or so I was in an awful mood. (I felt so bad it felt like my sperm lost!)

Finally, Ernie asked me: "What are you saying to yourself?"

I said: "I'm saying that I am such a jerk for doing that to that guy!"

"Stop it!" Ernie said. "I don't want anybody calling my husband a jerk! Not even my husband!"

"I didn't even realize I was doing that!" I replied.

I had been teaching this for three years and I fell into the lying feelings trap myself! I felt like a jerk. So I thought I was a jerk. So I said I was a jerk. And according to Ernie I had been acting like a jerk that week! All because I agreed with a lie.

You Have To Be On Constant Guard

Guard yourself and your family by guarding your thinking and your speaking. Your greatest enemy is not a burglar breaking into your house. Your greatest enemy is yourself and your lying feelings, your lying thoughts, and your lying statements. Be on guard.

If you could kick the person who is most responsible for the problems in your life, you wouldn't be able to sit down for a month. But don't verbally or mentally kick yourself. That is counter productive.

Instead be kind to yourself. You deserve it. Be kind to your children's parent. Be kind to your friend's friend. Be kind to your parent's son or daughter. Be kind to you.

You will grow and change a whole lot faster under a spirit of self-approval than under a spirit of self-criticism. You are a championship human being! Think it! Say it! Believe it! Feel it!

Here is a poem I wrote that can help you change your feelings from negative to positive!

Coach or Critic

A coach and a critic
Stood side by side,
Watching a contender's
Every stride.

"You won't make it!"
The critic yelled.
"You are so bad
You're going to get nailed!"

"Keep on going!"
The coach replied.
"You will win this race.
Don't be denied!"

Which voice was heard
I cannot say,
For you run this race
Every day.

Do you hear coach or critic?
The voice you choose
Will determine whether
You win or you lose!

Steve Simms

"We can so educate the will power that it will focus the thoughts upon the bright side of things, and upon objects that elevate the soul, thus forming a habit of happiness."

Orison Swett Marden

"Rosiness is not a worse window pane than gloomy gray when viewing the world."

Grace Paley

Chapter 8

Worglee--You're Expecting What?

Broken Enjoyers

SOME PEOPLE ACT LIKE their enjoyers are broken. That's a shame. People can live very well without an appendix or without tonsils, but not without an enjoyer! Without a working enjoyer, life becomes a bore.

An enjoyer is the organ that enables a person to experience joy in his life. Everybody is born with a healthy enjoyer. Notice how pleasure and delight come naturally to small children. Their enjoyers work extremely well.

But as people grow physically and mentally their enjoyers often shrink. People often lose their ability to enjoy life naturally. They become emotionally stiff, dull, and boring. Without an active enjoyer people turn to artificial stimulants and diversions in an attempt to find the pleasure that once came so naturally to them as children.

But satisfying, long-term pleasure cannot be found in a bottle or in an event! It must be released from within. There is no substitute for a healthy enjoyer–no artificial organ, no transplant.

Fortunately, everybody still has at least the remnant of an enjoyer which can with proper care and nourishment be revived. (Even a miserable valu-blinder has been seen to smile on very rare occasions.)

Would you like to build up your enjoyer? It has to be developed by use. The more you enjoy your life, the greater grows your capacity to enjoy it!

People want to experience the heights of ecstasy—the pinnacles of pleasure—and yet, they often haven't learned to enjoy real life itself. True pleasure begins with the simple things and grows with use. Have you exercised your enjoyer yet today?

The Challenge To Joy

When my daughter, Amelia, was three years old, she was dancing, humming, smiling, and laughing, as we waited in the check out line of a local grocery store. As it became our turn to check out, the clerk glared down at Amelia and growled, "Little girl, no one deserves to be that happy!"

I immediately knelt down beside Amelia and said, "Don't pay any attention to that grumpy lady. She doesn't know what she is talking about. You can be as happy as you want to be! You can even be way happier than you are right now!" Amelia smiled at me as if to say, "Thanks Dad!" and resumed her joyous celebration of life.

The clerk threw her head back and snarled at me. As she checked us out, she pounded down every grocery item extra hard. She was thoroughly disgusted with my daughter and me. "How dare we be happy?"

My little girl has brought a tremendous amount of happiness to my wife and me. We love her spontaneity, her spirit of celebration, and her ability to find pleasure in the simplest of things! She has the natural happiness of early childhood. Most young children have it (unless they are being raised in a harsh or abusive environment).

After observing young children, I have concluded we (human beings) are created to be happy! And yet as people get older we tend to lose our happiness. But is it any wonder? After all, we live in a negative world! Life is full of problems! Someone has said "The best way out of a problem is never to marry one in the first place." But that is easier said than done. I mean, if our problem isn't our spouse, it is our job (or lack of one), our health, our finances, and on and on!

We (human beings) have so many problems, that many people have falsely concluded, "People can't be happy, here in the real world! We don't deserve it!" So when something really good happens to someone, their friends and foes alike say: "Don't enjoy it too much. That's too good to last!"

When my wife and I got married we were delighted with each other! Most of our friends noticed our joy and shared the following words with us: "It won't last!" We almost panicked. We thought, "Let's not enjoy this wonderful feeling too much so we won't be so hurt when it goes away." But then we talked about it and we decided that we were going to be happy and fully enjoy each other, no matter how long it lasted. Seven years later I enjoy her more than ever. And she does me too! We have a lot of fun and problems, too. But problems don't have to kill joy! As Samuel Johnson said: "To strive with difficulties and to conquer them is the highest human felicity."

Nothing Is Too Good To Last So Fight For Delight

I believe nothing is too good to last! As human beings we were created to enjoy life. But this negative world and many of the people in it (valu-blinders like the grocery clerk) want to make us all sad. Therefore, being happy is a battle. It is a fight for delight!

But the battle is not to win over our circumstances. The battle for happiness is to establish a contented state of mind, a sense of well-being! It is an inside battle! Happiness is truly a matter of mind-over-matter—"if you don't mind, it don't matter!" When the inside battle is won, the battle is won! In other words, if you think you are happy, then you are happy! It is that simple.

Dale Carnegie put it this way: "There is one sure way to find it (happiness). That is by controlling your thoughts. Happiness doesn't depend on outward conditions. It depends on inward conditions."

Basically, happiness is a decision with follow through and hard mental work. A person decides: "Since I'm living anyway, I might as well enjoy it," and then he fights the inward battle to resist the negatives that attack him from himself and others. Every day above ground is truly a good day! It's great to be alive! My daughter knows that and it shows in her life! A lot of forces during her lifetime will try to make her sad. Every time she picks up a newspaper or turns on the radio or TV she will encounter bad news. But she is prepared. Amelia knows 1) that happiness is within her, 2) that she deserves (because of her value) and has a right to be happy, and 3) that the best thing she can do for this sad world is to spread her happiness and joy all around.

Carol S. Pearson said: "Joy is our birthright. We can attract joy as easily as we attract pain." Orison Swett Marden said: "Everyday should be a holiday, a day of joy and gladness, a day of supreme happiness."

Sidney B. Simon said: "I cannot find justification for feeling down, depressed, wounded, and withered...I feel the human being was meant to be sunny, giving, caring, thoughtful, delighted, and delightful—and a whole string of other positive things."

So What Is Worglee?

Amelia worglees! She expects the best and anticipates it with joy. Worglee is the opposite of worry. Let's look at a few definitions of worry and then we will look again at worglee.

Anna Brown Lindsay said: "Worry is spiritual nearsightedness; a fumbling way of looking at little things and magnifying their value." Corrie Ten Boom said: "Worry is a cycle of inefficient thoughts, whirling around a center of fear." And perhaps you can identify with John Lubbock who said: "A day of worry is more exhausting than a day of work."

My personal definition of worry is: worry is dread—it is mentally picturing the worst things and producing anxiety and torment by expecting them to happen to yourself or to people you love. Samuel Smiles put it this way: "Much of the fear that exists is the offspring of imagination, which creates the images or evils which may happen, but perhaps rarely do; and thus many persons who are capable of summoning up courage enough to grapple with and overcome real dangers, are paralyzed or thrown into consternation by those which are imaginary."

A Closer Look At Worglee

Worglee is the opposite. Lydia Sigourney said: "Life has, indeed, many ills, but the mind that views every object in its most cheering aspect, and every doubtful dispensation as replete with latent good, bears within itself a powerful and perpetual antidote." Amy Lowell said: "Let us be of good cheer, remembering that the misfortunes hardest to bear are those which never come."

Soren Kierkegaard said: "If I were to wish for anything, I should not wish for wealth and power, but for the passionate sense of potential, for the eye which, ever young and ardent, sees the possible. . . what wine is so sparkling, so fragrant, so intoxicating, as possibility!"

I define worglee as mentally picturing the best possible events about to happen to yourself and to those you love—then eagerly anticipating those events until they create great joy and happiness in your heart.

Examples of Worry And Worglee

Worry and worglee are really the same thing. The process is exactly the same. The only difference is the focus. Worry focuses on bad events that may happen in the future. Worglee focuses on good events that may happen in the future. So if you can worry, you (yes, you) can worglee!

The difference between worry and worglee is really nothing more than what you are saying to yourself and others—and what questions you are asking. Here are some examples.

Worry: What am I going to do if I lose my job? How will my family survive?

Worglee: What am I going to do if my boss doubles my salary? How will my family spend all that extra money?

Worry: What am I going to do if I get sick? How am I going to pay all the doctor bills? Will my family still love me? What if I get so sick that I die?

Worglee: What am I going to do if I stay healthy all my life? How will I spend all the money I save on medical bills? What exciting things will I get to do because I'm so healthy?

Worry: What if somebody I love gets really sick? How will I survive the pain of that?

Worglee: What if everybody in my family lives long and healthy lives? What fun things will I get to do with each of them?

Worry: What if someone breaks into my home? What if I can't cope with that?

Worglee: What if my home is the safest place in town? What if I get a safety award? How will I cope with all the love and attention I will be given?

Worry: What if the boss called that meeting on Monday morning to fire me? What if I am embarrassed in front of all my co-workers?

Worglee: What if the boss called that meeting on Monday morning to give me a raise and an award? Won't that be great if I am praised in front of all my co-workers?

Do you get the idea? Worry and worglee are the same, except one is focused on the positive possibilities and the other is focused on the negative possibilities.

Turn Worry Into Worglee

The next time you are worried, why not turn your worry into worglee? People sometimes tell me it feels silly to worglee. Well, let me ask you this. Just how intelligent is it to worry? Fred W. Newman said: "I got my ulcers and numerous ills from mountain climbing on molehills." How intelligent is that?

I've read that the English word "worry" comes from an old Anglo-Saxon word meaning "to strangle." And that's what worry does. It strangles your joy, your peace, your health.

E. Stanley Jones said: "Many live in dread of what is coming. Why should we? The unknown puts adventure into life. . .The unexpected around the corner gives a sense of anticipation and surprise." Samuel Smiles said: "The habit of viewing things cheerfully and of thinking about things hopefully may be made to grow in us like any other habits."

Worglee and worry are really nothing more than your belief about the future. Another name for worglee is hope!

Get Your Hopes Up With Worglee

Samuel Smiles said: "Hope is the companion of power and the mother of success; for whoso hopes strongly has within him the gift of miracles." So get your hopes up! Jesse Jackson said: "People need more hope than help. Keep hope alive." Get your hopes up!

Napoleon said: "A leader is a dealer in hope." Get your hopes up! Mother Teresa said: "We want to create hope for the person...we must give hope, always hope." Get your hopes up! Pearl S. Buck said: "To eat bread without hope is still slowly to starve to death." Get your hopes up! Orison Swett Marden said: "There is no medicine like hope, no incentive so great, and no tonic so powerful, as expectation of something tomorrow." Get your hopes up!

Charles Wagner said: "The most meager hope is nearer the truth than the most rational despair." Get your hopes up! Bernie S. Siegel, M.D. said: "Refusal to hope is nothing more than a decision to die." Get your hopes up! Sidney Smith defined hope: "Hope is the belief...that joy will come." Get your hopes up! John Calvin said: "When hope animates us there is a vigor in the whole body." Get your hopes up!

Next time you think everybody and everything is telling you to give up hope, read this section again! Here you will find a few folks who will tell you to get your hopes up!

A Boy And A Girl

I once heard a story about a little boy who was playing in the street with only one roller skate. He was having a great time, using his one skate like a scooter or like a skateboard.

A valu-blinder walked by and growled at the little boy: "Son, you're supposed to have two skates, not one!"

The little boy smiled and said: "I know I should have two skates, but you can have a whole lot of fun with one, if that's all you've got!"

Now that's worglee–enjoying what you do have and not worrying about what you don't have! And if a little boy can do it, then you can too!

I've heard a story about a little girl who told her mother one night: "I've had a really great day today!"

"I'm really glad," her mother replied. "But what made today different than yesterday when you were so worried and unhappy?"

The little girl thought for a minute and then said: "Yesterday I let my thoughts push me around, but today I decided to push around my thoughts!"

Now that's worglee–pushing your thoughts around in order to make yourself happy, rather than letting your thoughts push you around and make you worried and miserable. And if a little girl can do it, then you can too!

As Mahatma Gandhi said: "Always aim at purifying your thoughts and everything will be well. There is nothing more potent than thought."

Do Worglee. Be Happy!

You are a world class human being–an extraordinary winner–an exquisite example of a highly valuable person. Good things are coming your way. So get all worgleed about it. Celebrate your victory. Dance around with joy like my daughter, Amelia! Crank up your enjoyer. Kick your fears in their rears. Have a blast while you last. Spotlight positive possibilities. See something beautiful everywhere you look.

Obey Charles Dickens advice: "Reflect on your present blessings of which every man has plenty–not on your past misfortunes of which all men have some." Joyce Sequichie Hifler said: "The best comes when we release our hold on little cares, the voices that tell us how bad things are in the world—and just let peace seep in."

Martha Washington said: "I am determined to be cheerful and happy in whatever situation I may be, for I have learned from experience that the greater part of our happiness or misery depends on our dispositions and not on our circumstances."

You are too valuable to worry. Now you don't have to, because you know how to worglee!

Mary Crowley summed it up when she said: "There is magic in belief, but 90 percent of all people utilize this magic the wrong way by believing in the bad things that can happen—instead of imagining and expecting great things to happen."

"The power of self-help will gradually grow, and in proportion to a man's self-respect."

Samuel Smiles

"A bad habit never disappears miraculously; it is an undo it yourself project."

Abigail Van Buren

Chapter 9

Self-Tech

You're Worth Working On

NOTHING IN THE WORLD is worth working on more than you are! Because of your tremendous value, the best use of your thoughts, energy, time, and effort is to invest in improving yourself! You can work to make improvements in your home. You can strive to improve your work place. You can struggle to improve your financial status. But if you really want to work on something important, work on yourself.

Self-tech is the scientific and systematic approach to self-improvement. It is knowledge and technology applied to you, by you. Self-tech is the steady attempt to recognize, experience, and enhance your personal value.

To a large degree, self-tech is common sense applied to yourself in an uncommon way. Self-tech is taking the free information and knowledge about how to effectively operate yourself (which most people ignore) and consistently using it to make yourself even better.

Self-tech says: "As a human being I am the most advanced, sophisticated, complicated, powerful, and important computer on the planet and I am going to learn to use myself to produce and run all the good programming I can. I am going to make me be all I can be."

Edwin T. Freedley said: "He who seizes the grand idea of self-cultivation, and solemnly resolves upon it, will find that idea, that resolution burning like fire within him, and ever putting him upon his own improvement. He will find it removing difficulties; searching out or making means, giving courage for despondency, and strength for weakness."

The Goals Of Self-Tech

What are the specific goals of self-tech? Ultimately what can self-tech accomplish? Here is a sampling of the results of effective self-tech: joy, happiness, inner peace, confidence, self-esteem, love, kindness, self-respect, assurance, motivation, value, significance, self-control, strength, hope, enthusiasm, encouragement, excitement, cheerfulness, character, fortitude, optimism, gratification, patience, compassion, dedication, elation, perseverance, integrity, boldness, power, resolution, self-belief, acceptance, steadiness, composure, worglee, glee, empathy, balance, courage, commitment, integrity, dignity, stamina, tolerance, service, exhilaration, effectiveness, diligence, delight, honor, faithfulness, self-acceptance, poise, purpose, vitality, sincerity, loyalty, morality, comfort, stability, determination, energy, satisfaction, endurance, recognition, abundance, jollity, principle, persistence, fulfillment, honesty, pleasure, durability.

What would your life be like if you used self-tech to produce these emotions and qualities in your life? Well, you deserve these qualities and emotions in abundance! And they are what you and everybody else on the planet are looking for.

People say they want money and wealth—but what do they really want? Stacks of green stuff? Not really. They want the security, peace, comfort, power, self-esteem, and other positive qualities they believe the money will give them.

People say they want success—but what do they really want? They want the power, accomplishment, gratification, sense of well being, and other qualities they believe the success will give them.

So here's my question. Why not go directly for the qualities? Self-tech cuts to the heart of the matter.

James Freeman Clarke said: "Progress, in the sense of acquisition is something, but progress in the sense of being, is a great deal more. To grow, higher, deeper, wider as the years go on; to conquer difficulties, and acquire more and more power; to feel all one's faculties unfolding, and truth descending into the soul—this makes life worth living."

Self-Tech In Rugby, Tennessee

I recently spent two nights in Historic Rugby, Tennessee—Pioneer Cottage to be exact—and stepped back in time into the 1880's. Rugby is just past the boundary of the Eastern Time Zone when you are headed east on Highway 52 in East Tennessee, but the time change feels like a hundred years rather than one hour.

My lodging, Pioneer Cottage, was built in 1878, the first building constructed in the English colony of Rugby, Tennessee. It is a rustic, two story, three bedroom, "carpenter Gothic" house, located about three feet from the highway. There is almost no traffic except for three or four large trucks that buzz by every hour, abruptly breaking the silence.

The other buildings in Rugby include a store, a cafe, a church, a school (converted into a museum and visitor center), and a library. Most of them are original, 1880's structures with a couple of reproductions.

Rugby was founded by a famous English author, Thomas Hughes, as a social experiment and an attempt to create a new society. It quickly grew to about 400 residents, but since it was located in a sparsely populated, wilderness area, many of the new residents became discouraged and left. By the beginning of this century, Rugby was a tiny hamlet with few people and has remained so ever since.

What brought me to Rugby? Well, it is a nice place to visit and a great way to experience "living history." But my primary interest was the library. When the town was founded, publishers from across the United States and Great Britain sent Thomas Hughes copies of their books. Today the petite "Thomas Hughes Library" contains 7000 volumes of books published before 1899. Stepping into the library is to experience the early days of Rugby. Everything is just as it was 100 years ago.

As a motivational speaker and self-help author, when I first heard about the Rugby collection of antique books, I couldn't wait to explore them. I called Historic Rugby and asked for permission to use the library. I am grateful they granted my request.

I was privileged to spend two days in that old, dusty library thumbing through hundreds of volumes of Nineteenth Century wisdom. Some of the self-tech treasures I discovered include:

"No man can be wholly unhappy who is accustomed to look for beauty in nature and in human life. He has a joy which never wearies." James Freeman Clarke–1882.

"It is he who resolves to succeed, who at every fresh rebuff begins resolutely again, that reaches the goal." Edwin T. Freedley–1879

"There are some things that cost no money, things, indeed that cannot by possibility be bought under a standard of money value, but are the dearest things that a man can purchase." Joseph Farrell–1877.

"Happiness consists in the enjoyment of little pleasures scattered along the common path of life, which in the eager

search for some great and exciting joy, we are apt to overlook."
Samuel Smiles–1859.

"Keep steadily before you that all true success depends
at last upon yourself." Theodore Munger–1881.

"He who resolves upon doing a thing by that very
resolution often scales the barriers to it, and secures its
achievement." Samuel Smiles.

"In order to do anything in this world that is worth
doing, we must not stand shivering on the bank, and thinking
of the cold and the danger, but jump in and scramble through
as well as we can." Sydney Smith.

"If solid happiness we prize,
Within our breast this jewel lies;
The world has nothing to bestow;
From our own selves our joys must flow."
N. Cotton.

After two days, I had to return to the present–the high
tech age of cellular phones, Internet surfing, and TV channel
flipping. Yet with all our sophisticated means of com-
munication I have yet to find in our generation, the degree of
wisdom, comfort, encouragement, and self-tech that I found in
Rugby, Tennessee.

Here is a collection of the very best self-tech ideas I
found in Rugby:

Rugby's Nineteenth Century Wisdom
For Twenty-First Century Success

Make time yield fruits. Cultivate a good principle.
Strengthen a good habit. Be energetic. Educate yourself.
Learn something worthy of being known. Seize and improve
opportunities for action and effort. Seize the grand idea of
self-cultivation (self-tech).

Will strongly and decisively. Exercise self-discipline, self-control, and self-respect. Have confidence in yourself. Hope strongly. Look up. Aspire. Make an energetic attempt. Feel you can. Cultivate yourself. Transform possibility into reality. Attempt and accomplish the best and most useful things. Scale the barriers to accomplishment.

Be cheerful. Create your own happiness. Extract joy from life. Enjoy little pleasures. Release your capacity for enjoyment. Enjoy the things that cost no money. Hold a steady purpose. Jump in and scramble through the best you can. Turn your possibilities into powers. Fix your floating life. Look for beauty in nature and in human life. Carry about good thoughts. Make other people happy.

Resolve and determine to advance. Cultivate energy, invincible determination, and an honest purpose. Try. At every fresh rebuff, begin resolutely again. Succeed through failure. Work hard—exert yourself. Make the best of every-thing. Hope for the best. Think the best. Evoke energy in others. Anticipate intensely. Reflect, appreciate, see and feel with your heart. Carry about good thoughts. Master your habits. Make happiness habitual. Make progress in the sense of being.

Self-Tech For Less Stress

You may have seen the chart in stress management books or seminars. It is a list of dozens of negative events that range from mildly inconvenient to major tragedies. Each event is given a number value with the mild ones having low numbers and the worst tragedy ranked at 100.

You are instructed to check all the "stressful" things that have happened to you in the past year and then add up your total points. If that number exceeds 100, you better bail out of some things, because you are STRESSED!

The problem is, most people's scores exceed 100 and some soar toward a thousand. It appears we are condemned for life to the pressure cooker. I know it is not news, but life today takes place in a stress conducive environment!

Often there is not much we can do about our high pressure circumstances. As nice as it sounds, running away to Tahiti is not a valid option for most of us.

So how can we use self-tech to reduce our stress even when we can't fix our circumstances? The keys to genuine, long-term stress reduction are the Seven Self-Tech Characteristics of Peaceful (Low-Stress) People.

The Seven Self-Tech Characteristics of Peaceful (Low-Stress) People

1) Peaceful people are mentally tough! They maintain inner peace by resisting and driving away anxiety producing thoughts. Not that they have their heads in the sand. Peaceful people deal with the negative realities of life, but they don't wallow in them. They do what they can, and then they use self-tech to stubbornly toss fear, worry, frustration, disappointment, resentment, self-pity, depression, and other gremlins from their mind!

2) Peaceful people limit their responsibility. They have resigned as general manager of the universe. They realize that they cannot control the thoughts and behaviors of other people, so they let go. Peaceful people take responsibility for their own thoughts, words, and behaviors; nothing more!

3) Peaceful people learn and use effectiveness skills. They organize, delegate, avoid procrastination, know how to say "no," prioritize, avoid perfectionism, use time saving tools. In short, peaceful people work smart. And when a task is done they are done with the task.

4) Peaceful people take physical and mental breaks. They know how to relax, to unwind, to play, to pray, to laugh,

to be silly, to stop and watch a tree grow. They don't spend hours during the day avoiding work, but they do pause often to sharpen their mental and emotional ax. And sometimes they even take a vacation!

5) Peaceful people don't chase rabbits. They don't drop a high-priority task to pursue an urgent, low-priority task. An exciting sports discussion around the water cooler doesn't seduce them into postponing an important task.

6) Peaceful people focus on one bite at a time. Have you ever seen someone put corn, peas, steak, and mashed potatoes in his mouth at the same time? What does it taste like? I bet he doesn't have any idea. It's just a blob of stuff. Although few of us eat food that way, that's exactly how many of us live our lives. We stuff them full of everything at once. Peaceful people live in compartments. When they are doing one thing, they are not thinking about something else. Peaceful people focus.

7) Peaceful people have faith in God. This is pragmatic, not religious. How would you feel at forty thousand feet in an airplane with no pilot? That's how people feel in a world with no God. Peaceful people avoid that feeling. They nurture and develop their spiritual life and the sense of inner peace it produces.

Maybe you cannot de-stress your environment, but you can de-stress your mind and emotions by developing the Seven Self-Tech Characteristics of Peaceful People. Sure it is hard work to use self-tech, but it is worth it!

What To Do When You Are At The End Of Your Rope

You may have seen the post card that reads: "I deserve this nervous breakdown, I've worked for it, and by golly I'm going to have it!" Admittedly that's not the best of attitudes, but it is a common human experience. As a professional "Encouragement Engineer" I have to confess that there are times I just plain don't want to feel good. I just don't want to use self-tech.

I mean, sometimes I get tired of being positive. And sometimes it seems like some of my goals and dreams have been delayed so long they are never going to happen. I teeter on the brink of downright discouragement and can't think of any reason not to dive in.

Those are frightening moments. As we have seen, throwing in the emotional towel and wallowing in self-pity is not really a very attractive option. But how do you move back from the abyss of depression, when you are not even sure you want to? How do you motivate yourself to keep on believing when all you want to do is "fall apart?" Here are a few self-tech ideas that have helped me turn myself around, even when I felt completely unmotivated.

1) Don't salt your wounds! You're hurting, but don't add to your pain by attacking yourself, your family and associates, or your fate. Drop the accusations; put off the put-downs. Accept your struggle as normal. Simon Peter said: "Do not be surprised at the painful trial you are suffering, as if something strange were happening to you." You are not in a unique situation. You are not weird. It is normal to have occasional struggles with despair. So go easy on yourself.

2) Change your focus. Stall your emotions by distracting yourself with a non-self-destructive activity. Do something that's not part of your daily routine. Go to a movie. Call someone you haven't talked with in ages (I just called my old friend Marlon Raines). Play with a child. Go for a walk or drive. Write something (that's what I'm doing now). Help somebody. Go to bed early (I did that one last night).

3) Use fear. Fear is a powerful motivator. Let the fear of even greater discouragement get hold of you. What if you do completely give up? What if you become so depressed you cannot even function? What if you slip into self-destructive behaviors: alcohol abuse, drugs, anger, suicide? What if you

cause intense pain for someone you love? Let fear cause you to care. Someone has said: "Only giants in determination can be king of self." The fear of giving up will energize you to overcome and make you an inner giant.

Here's a poem that causes me fear:

If you have left your dreams behind,
If hope is cold,
If you no longer look ahead,
If your ambition fires are dead,
Then you are old.

Anon.

4) Face reality. You're depressed. Admit it. You're discouraged. Go ahead and acknowledge it. You're disappointed. Accept that, too. Things are bad. OK.

Be careful, however, not to overstate the truth. You're depressed, but you're not worthless. You're discouraged, but you're not totally defeated. You're disappointed, but all is not lost. Some things are indeed bad, but some things are still good.

Face reality as it really is. Don't exaggerate to the extremes of either: pretending you don't have a problem or imagining that all you have is problems. Face the facts. Try to avoid your opinions. Remember, don't let your emotions overstate reality.

5) Ride out the storm. Everything changes. The circumstances you are depressed about today will eventually change, too. The tide will turn. This pain you are feeling will pass away. Things will look up. The sun will come out tomorrow! These are not just clichés, but powerful, self-tech thoughts! Use them! Say them to yourself and say them out loud until you are sick of hearing them; then say them some more.

Buy a small, thumb-operated counter from a sporting goods store and count your positive thoughts. Register 5,000 positive thoughts a day on your counter. When you are at the end of your rope you have two options: 1) let go; or 2) tie a knot and hang on! Continuously choose option number 2, even when you don't feel like it.

6) Get help. Talk to a friend. Join a twelve step group. Call a crisis hot-line. Call a prayer line. Talk to God. Get professional help... Go to a counselor, a pastor, or a doctor, or a hospital. Always remember, you are too valuable to give up!

In this chapter, we've only looked at a very few self-tech ideas. If you would like to explore dozens of additional self-tech recipes, such as: "Seven Benefits of a Happy Attitude," "Eight Practical Steps to Problem-Solving," and "Eight Ways to Enjoy Your Work;" I refer you to my book, *Mindrobics: How To Be Happy For The Rest Of Your Life*. As for now, let's turn the page and take a look at Self-Value.

Steve Simms

"You radiate to the world the way you feel about yourself."
Lucy Freeman

"No man can be happy unless he feels his life in some way important."
Bertrand Russell

Chapter 10

Self-Value

What Are You Worth To You?

SOMEONE HAS SAID THAT self-value is the value you have left after all the value other people give to you has gone away. Joyce Sequichie Hifler said: "Our worth is not measured by what someone else thinks—but by what we think. One hour of self-approval does more for us than years of waiting to hear that we measure up."

Harold H. Bloomfield said: "You can experience enormous pleasure in your day-to-day activity if you give yourself permission to appreciate your own magnificence." And Samuel Smiles said: "Self-respect is the noblest garment with which a man may clothe himself, the most elevating feeling with which the mind can be inspired."

Dr. William Glasser said: "All psychological problems, from the slightest neurosis to the deepest psychosis, are merely symptoms of the frustration of the fundamental need for a sense of personal worth."

Avoiding Self-Dislike

The opposite of self-value is self-dislike. Self-dislike is more than just an innocent waste of time. It is very destructive.

Self-dislike robs us of our own abilities. Orison Swett Marden said: "Perhaps there is no other one thing which keeps so many people back as their low estimate of themselves. They are more handicapped by their limiting thought, by their foolish convictions of inefficiency, than by almost anything else."

Self-dislike causes us to be unkind to others. "Sidney J. Harris said: "The amount of pain we inflict upon others is directly proportional to the amount we feel within." Dorothy Carnegie said: "People who hate everything and everybody, who mistreat and dislike their fellow men, are merely expressing their own frustrations and profound self-disgust."

Self-dislike causes us to be over critical of others. Dorothy Carnegie also said: "Excessive fault finding...is one of the symptoms displayed by people who do not like themselves."

Self-dislike causes other people not to like us. Arlene Raven said: "The way in which we think of ourselves has everything to do with how our world sees us."

Self-dislike causes us to want to put ourselves down. And self-put-downs have a way of becoming reality for us. A.L. Kitselman said: "The words 'I am...' are potent words; be careful what you hitch them to. The thing you're claiming has a way of reaching back and claiming you."

Self-dislike lowers your morale. Self-dislike depletes your energy. Self-dislike prevents you from using self-tech to take constructive steps in your life. Self-dislike produces self-cruelty.

So why do people get stuck in self-dislike? Because as bad as self-dislike is, some people choose to like not liking themselves.

The Perceived (But False) Rewards Of Self-Dislike

People who don't value themselves mistakenly feel (those lying feelings again) that there are benefits to not liking themselves. They mistakenly think:

1) Low self-esteem is a built in excuse for failure. Because they don't like themselves, they believe the lie that says they will never have to try to make something out of their lives.

2) Self-dislike is protection from the pain of rejection. Because they have already rejected themselves, they mistakenly feel they have taken the sting out of rejection from others.

3) Self-rejection stops change. Because they have discarded their potential, they falsely believe they won't have to change.

4) Low self-esteem causes others to give them a lot of pity, sympathy, and attention. Because they have chosen to complain and whine, they wallow in negative attention from other people. They feel like the sympathy they get by manipulation is genuine love. They fail to see that the people around them don't like their behavior.

5) Self-dislike opens the door to blame others. Because they feel so helpless, people who don't like themselves feel like every problem in their lives must be someone else's fault.

6) Low-self esteem frees them from responsibility. Because they believe the lie that they are worthless and can't do anything right, and convey that belief about themselves to others, most people don't expect them to do much.

7) It is easier to put themselves down than it is to try to get up. Because they feel powerless, they agree with the lies that come to their mind, rather than trying to fight them.

It's Time To Dislike Self-Dislike

I don't like self-dislike. I don't like it in me and I don't like it in you. This book is my attempt to help reduce the level of self-dislike in our world. So how can you reduce your level of self-dislike?

Pretend you are a spy eavesdropping on your conversations with other people and on your own internal dialogue. Notice what you are saying. Take yourself literally. Do you mean what you say?

Paul Bunyan Story

Our words reveal how we really feel about ourselves. And yet the words we use are such habits that we often don't even realize what we are saying.

There is a story about the legendary logger, Paul Bunyan, I read years ago. I've forgotten the exact details, but here is my version. One particularly cold winter Paul was working with a big mean logger named Big Jim. Big Jim was so negative and foul mouthed that he offended all of the other loggers. He even offended tough ole Paul Bunyan.

Big Jim was so mean and strong, however, that everyone was afraid to say anything to him about his attitude and his language--everyone that is except Paul Bunyan. Paul told Big Jim that his words were causing great distress in the logging camp. But Jim just laughed and said: "If they can't handle it, let them leave. Besides, I'm not saying anything that (expletive deleted) bad!"

Paul was amazed. Jim was constantly saying self-destructive things and yet he was so used to it, he no longer noticed the harm his words caused.

A few days later the blizzard of the century hit the logging camp. Paul Bunyan used the bad weather to his advantage. He followed Big Jim around. Jim cursed the weather, his fate, the other loggers, and himself. Because of the extreme cold, however, his words froze solid. So Paul Bunyan picked them up and stored them for the rest of the winter.

When the spring thaw came, Paul got Big Jim and brought him to the pile of frozen words. As they began to thaw, Big Jim was shocked. "Who said all those terrible things!" he demanded. "I'll beat the (expletive deleted) out of them!"

"You did!" said Paul Bunyan. "Those are your words, Big Jim, and nobody else's."

Big Jim sat down and put his head in his hands. He sat there in shock, while all his worst words and phrases of that winter played back for him to hear. After the last word thawed, Jim got up, picked up his ax, and said: "I'm going to the woods."

Three weeks later, Big Jim came walking into camp, smiling from ear to ear. He grabbed a logger's hand, shook it, and said: "It's a great day, isn't it!" From that day on, everything that Big Jim said exuded encouragement!

When Paul Bunyan asked Big Jim what he did in the woods for those three weeks, he said: "I listened to the words in my head. And I didn't like them either. So I changed them. And when I changed them I felt so much better I had to come back to camp so everybody could hear my new words and feel better too!"

Are your words spreading self-dislike? Really listen to yourself—pay close attention to the literal meaning of the things you say and the things you think. Awareness is a powerful tool for changing self-dislike to self-esteem.

So What Do You Like About You?

Make a list of the things you like about yourself. Before you answer, "Nothing," think about it. Do you like your eyes? Or would you rather do without them? Do you like having arms and legs? Do you like having lungs? Breathing is pretty nice, isn't it? Do you like being able to read? That is a very likeable ability. Do you like being able to speak English? Billions of people can't do that!

Sure there are a few things that you don't like about yourself. That is all right. Forget about the few things you don't like about you and concentrate on the hundreds of things you do like about you.

If I wanted to use up dozens of pages of this book I could list hundreds of things that I am sure you like about you—instead here are a few: your hands, your finger nails, your elbows, your heart, your brain, your ability to walk, your ability to sit up and take nourishment, and I could go on and on! I know you like those things about yourself, so think about them. And quit beating yourself up with the few things that you don't like about you.

Seven Ways To Like Yourself More

In my book, *Mindrobics: How To Be Happy For The Rest Of Your Life*, I have a chapter called: "Seven Ways To Like Yourself Better." I've received such good response from people about how these ideas have helped them, that I am going to include a brief summary of those principles in this chapter on "Self-Value."

1) Don't compare yourself with others. Here are a couple of recent quotes I have found on comparison. Max Ehrmann said: "If you compare yourself with others you may become vain or bitter, for always there will be greater and lesser persons than yourself."

And Jamie Lee Curtis said: "For years I stopped reading beauty magazines because I couldn't look at one without wanting to blow my brains out. How can those women look so good?" Comparing is destructive of your self-esteem so don't do it!

2) Stay in line with your conscience and moral values. When you violate your conscience you trample your sense of self-value.

3) Forgive yourself. Let go of your past failures and regrets. Everybody else has forgotten them, so you may as well, too.

4) Separate personal worth from performance. You don't have to be perfect to be valuable. You don't even have to be very good. Your sperm won so you already are valuable. Quit trying to earn what you already have.

5) Accept compliments from other people. When someone gives you a compliment, don't reject it by making an excuse. Instead receive that compliment by saying: "Thank you."

6) Give yourself compliments. Notice what you do right and acknowledge it. You don't need to brag to others, just compliment yourself in your own mind.

7) Use the affirmation: "I like myself." I've even put it to music. Some times I sing it over and over. I've even been known to sing it in a speech. Go ahead and say, "I like myself." Say it often whether you feel it or not and sooner or later you will begin to feel it.

Self-Value Sets You Free

When you really value yourself you are free from competition. You don't have to beat everybody else to prove your worth. You already know it. Whether you win, lose, or don't even show up, you feel good about you.

Self-value is wonderful. You are somebody. Maybe the whole world hasn't recognized that fact, but it is time you recognized it. It's a fact.

When lying feelings knock on your door to tell you that you are of little value, don't answer—instead read the next chapter, Valu-Soup For Your Soul!

Steve Simms

"Live as if you like yourself, and it may happen."
Marge Piercy

"I have discovered the ultimate goal in life is to be your own best friend—and only after you have befriended yourself can you be a friend to others."
Shantidasa

Chapter 11

Valu-Soup For Your Soul-- 11 Original Stories To Help You Experience Your Value

Valu-Soup No. 1–N.R. Winner

N.R. WINNER HAS HAD his ups and downs. There were many years early in his adult life when outward success eluded him. Oh, he earned a "living." As some folks say: "He got by." But often times were tough!

Through it all N.R. fought to overcome his difficulties. He tried his best to improve his circumstances and to make his life a model of success. Yet despite all his efforts he encountered set back after set back. The conditions of his life seemed to say that he would never be anything but "average."

Still despite the frustrations and disappointments, N.R. Winner continued to try to rearrange his circumstances. He had a dream and he wasn't a quitter.

But as the years went by he finally began to realize that his outward efforts were not enough. And somewhere along the way he made a great discovery—that real success is not without, but within! When the inside battle is won, the battle is won!

N.R. had been fighting for years on the wrong front—battling to change his circumstances rather than struggling to change himself.

So N.R. switched his effort. He began to fight his thoughts and to rearrange his attitudes. He began to drive out doubt, depression, and despair. He fought against anxiety, self-dislike, bitterness, and resentment. And he discovered that positive thinking is not an easy thing to do.

But N.R. persisted and gradually he began to win within—to feel peaceful, happy, content, successful, confident, secure!

At last N.R. Winner realized that unpleasant circumstances and set backs could not hold him back—that he was free in his mind! So he began to vividly live his dreams in his thoughts and imagination. He got so involved with his struggle to win within that he began to forget about all his outward misery.

N.R. began to quote Paul of Tarsus saying: "I have learned in whatever state I am therewith to be content."

And almost without noticing it, N.R. Winner's outward circumstances began to change! His business prospered and he became wealthy. His friendships became strong and fulfilling. His relationship with his wife became rich. People began to look to N.R. as a role model, to ask his advice, and to invite him to speak at meetings.

N.R. Winner's advice on how to be successful in life is simple. Still, many people miss it. He says: "First win within, and then without a doubt, you'll win without! Be an inner winner!"

If you are determining your personal value solely by your outward circumstances and by other people's opinions of you, then you probably will never believe you are of tremendous value. To dramatically experience your value look within to reason, logic, and spirituality.

Valu-Soup No. 2–Lucille's Self-Portrait

"That'll be $29.23."

Lucille filled out a check and handed it to the cashier.

"I'll need to see your driver's license, Ma'am."

Lucille complied, holding her thumb over the photograph.

"Now Ma'am, how am I going to know if this is your driver's license unless I can see the picture?" the clerk asked as she grabbed Lucille's billfold and held it up to her face. "Are you sure this is really you?" the clerk asked.

"It's me." Lucille looked down and snarled.

"Oh, uh, don't feel bad. Uh, you look a whole lot better in person," the clerk said. Lucille silently gathered up her things and rushed to her car, mad and humiliated because she didn't like the picture in her wallet.

Like Lucille, you too carry around a picture of yourself. It hangs prominently in the private gallery of your thoughts. It is not a photograph. It is a painting–a self-portrait. The brush strokes consist of the thoughts and opinions you have about you–the way you see yourself.

And like Lucille, you may be ashamed of the picture of yourself that you carry in your mind. You may even try to hide it. But your self-portrait eventually pops out for all the world to see. It shows through the things you say and do.

That's because the way you paint yourself in your mind determines how you feel and how you act. Paint yourself as an important person who is making a difference in the world and that is how you will be. Paint yourself as a nobody and you will feel inferior, insecure, rejected, dejected, and neglected.

If you have an embarrassing and distorted self-painting hanging in the gallery of your thoughts, take it down and hang up a masterpiece–a self-portrait that shows the wonderful person that you are. Then you will feel great about your personal value.

Valu-Soup No. 3—A Suffering Man

The man was screaming. It was obvious that he was in terrible pain! Tears were running down his face and he was shaking.

"Oh! Help me! Somebody please help me! This thing is killing me!" he cried. In his left hand he tightly clinched a red hot piece of metal. It bore the initials "PP."

"Drop it!" I shouted. "That metal is burning your hand up!"

"I know it! Oh! It hurts so bad! But how do I get free from this?" He looked at the metal. Smoke came from his hand. His flesh sizzled! So I kicked his hand and the glowing metal fell to the ground. But it was too late. The flesh inside his hand was all burned away and the exposed bones were burned black!

Why would anyone hold on to a hot piece of metal like that—causing himself excruciating pain and permanent damage to his body? Surely nothing like that ever really happens. (Maybe I just made this story up.)

But the story is true. Many people are tightly gripping a "PP"—causing themselves untold agony and crippling their bodies—torturing themselves with a red hot "PP"—past pain! And how desperately they need to drop it. But how?

Just drop it! Let it go! Quit thinking about it! Quit fuming over it! It is that simple. So stop it.

And yet many people (maybe even you) refuse to drop past pain. Instead they nurture it and cause it to grow by concentrating on their disappointments, failures, and injustices. They develop red hot bitterness, resentment, anger, and hatred—and their peace, joy, and love, slowly and painfully burn up.

I've heard these pitiful people say: "I can't forget! I can't forgive! I can't let go! After what he did to me!" And yet "what he did" is very small in comparison to what the person did to himself by holding that burning hurt until it seared his very soul.

Just let it go! Don't ruin your experience of your value by clinging to past pain.

Valu-Soup No.4–Huntley Hunt's Hunting Handbook

*"Huntley Hunt's All Purpose Hunting Handbook–*only a buck!" Dan Aimless thought. "Now that's an offer I can't refuse."

Dan took the book off the discount table and walked, beaming, to the check out stand. He loved to find a bargain. In fact, finding discounts was about the only thing in life that motivated Dan, that is until he read Huntley Hunt's book.

Over night Dan became a hunting enthusiast! The book taught him about camping, hiking, marksmanship, outdoor clothing, tracking, how to build blinds and stands. The more he read, the more excited Dan became.

Finally he could stand no more. Dan went out and bought all the supplies that the book said he needed. He loaded up his pick-up and headed for the woods with his fourteen year old son, John Aimless.

That night neither father or son slept much. The ground was hard and uncomfortable, but even if they had been in a five-star hotel, they wouldn't have slept because of the anticipation of their first hunt!

Up before sunrise, dressed in camouflage, they began to prowl through the woods. "Dad, this isn't as much fun as I thought it would be." John Aimless said later that afternoon.

"We've just got to give it time, Son," Dan said. Meanwhile they continued to wander around, guns loaded and ready, looking right and left.

After two days of snooping around the woods they never even fired a shot. They were both exhausted as they loaded up the truck and began the trip home.

John interrupted the silence: "Dad, what exactly were we trying to kill out there, anyway?"

"Well, I don't really know. I guess I was just hunting for whatever I could find," answered Don Aimless.

Now this is a silly story, isn't it? No one ever goes hunting without knowing what they are hunting! (How else would they know if they found it?) But millions of people, like Don and John Aimless, are wandering aimlessly through life, without goals and dreams; without a vision of what they want to accomplish with their amazing lives.

Solomon said: "Where there is no vision, the people perish." Depression and discouragement, loneliness and anxiety, come easily to people who have no motivating purpose for their life.

Many people casually browse through life, accepting any blessings they might accidently stumble across, but unwilling to decide what it is they really want. A few people decide exactly what they want and hunt for it with great effort—and they usually find it!

The first step to accomplishment is: Know what you are hunting for!

Valu-Soup No. 5—What's Your Cud?

What's your cud? What do you enjoy chewing on, like an old cow—chewing gum, a blade of grass, candy, tobacco? Ping! Be sure to hit the spittoon or trash can. Thunk! I met a fellow once who likes to chew on plastic straws.

"I don't chew cud!" you may be thinking. Well maybe you don't actually chew cud, but you do churn things around in your mind from time to time. We might say you chew on thought cud.

116

Some people chew on negative thoughts. They pout and brood and sulk, ever so fine, savoring all the bitter juices that life has to offer. Many times during the day they cough up sour thoughts—hashing and rehashing them—continually making themselves madder or sadder. Negative thoughts make lousy mental cud. They cause "stinkin' thinking." And if not brought under control negative thoughts will spread misery and depression throughout a person's entire personality—creating an "old sour puss."

But positive thoughts produce the opposite effect. People who mentally chew on positive words and thoughts feel good and enthusiastic about life. Solomon put it this way: "Pleasant words are as a honeycomb, sweet to the soul and health to the bones." Chew on that thought for awhile!

You can tell what a person's mental cud is, just by looking at him. It shows on his face, in what he says, and in how he acts. People who frown, glare, slump, whine, complain, mumble, and pout, chew regularly on bad mental cud. But people who smile, laugh, compliment, help other people, and exhibit confidence and enthusiasm for living, are chewing on pleasant mental cud!

As Col. WM. C. Hunter said: "Fixed thought inevitably molds a man and makes him a creature of his thought picture."

You had better choose your mental cud very carefully! Everybody knows what you are thinking. Your mental cud is showing! So don't be careless about your cud! Continually chew on the good mental cud and spit out the bad. Then you will have a new appreciation of your personal value!

Steve Simms

"A person really believes something when he acts as if it were so."

Seneca

"It is a psychological fact that man always conforms to the image he holds of himself. Change his image and you change his actions, his reactions, his environment, his world."

Jack Holland

Chapter 12

Valu-Soup For Your Soul--Part 2 — The Rest Of The Stories

Valu-Soup No. 6–Mable Jernigan's Invisible Attack

MABLE JERNIGAN STRAINED AS she lifted her sack of groceries off the check out stand. "May I help you with your groceries?" the sacker asked.

"No thank you, Sonny. I'm a tough ole gal. I can carry one sack of groceries." Mable replied.

But this sack was extra heavy. The store had a special offer–six cans of green beans for a dollar–and Mable bought three dollars worth, plus her usual gallon of milk, half gallon of orange juice, and five large cans of cat food.

Mable started walking toward her car squeezing the bag tighter. As she felt it slowly slipping down her body she threw her legs into high gear and began to race against the invisible force of gravity. But just as she reached her car the bag collapsed and gravity won as tin cans bounced around her feet–fortunately missing her toes.

Mable looked at the empty bag with the blown out bottom that she was now holding in her hands. Then she flung that bag into the wind and it began to scoot like a sailboat, across the parking lot and toward the trash bins.

Mable's accident has been immortalized in a short, original, non-famous poem by me:

> *"A brown paper bag collapses,*
> *Yielding to the invisible force,*
> *That constantly strives,*
> *To seize its contents.*
> *Empty! Now the mutilated bag,*
> *Is a prisoner,*
> *Of the wind!"*

The moral is that there are invisible forces (like temptation, anger, addictions, peer pressure, bitterness, "genetic tendencies," etc.) that are constantly trying to get you to drop the contents of your character. But if you surrender and your moral bottom falls out, you are going to be blown around—a prisoner of invisible powers.

Col. WM. C. Hunter put it this way: "He who listlessly drifts with the tide, yielding to every appetite or passion, will soon dash a broken wreck on the sullen rocks that lurk unseen in the river of life!"

As a championship human being, you are too valuable to self-destruct—you are too good for that! Pick up the sagging elements of your character and fight your invisible foes. In the fight for right, your experience of your value will grow stronger!

Valu-Soup No. 7–The Two Tude Brothers

Have you heard about the two Tude brothers? Atta and Alta? What a pair! Mrs. Tude was really proud of her two sons.

Atta was the oldest. Because he had never been disciplined he was completely unpredictable. One day he might be happy, the next day sad. Sometimes he was friendly; other times mean. You could never tell about Atta Tude! Whew! Just trying to keep up with Atta was enough to give you whip lash!

Funny thing though, wherever Atta went Alta was sure to follow. Those two Tude brothers stuck together like a dog and its tail. When Atta Tude said jump, Alta Tude asked "How high?" and then jumped! Alta could never make a decision on his own. He always copied his big brother Atta!

Like Mrs. Tude, you also have two "tudes," your attitude and your altitude. And the old cliche is true, your attitude always determines your altitude!

You will never climb any higher in life than you feel and believe you can. When your attitude goes up, your altitude–your position in life–will soar. If your attitude crashes, your altitude will soon follow.

Many people ignore their attitude and let it run wild. They wonder why they have such trouble trying to climb the ladder to a higher altitude of success in life. But as long as they allow their attitude to wildly flop around like a loose water hose, their altitude will always be shaky, unstable, and on the verge of falling.

Why? Because in order to go higher in life, you must first go higher in thought! To be secure in your circumstances, you must first be secure in your mind!

It is not easy to discipline your attitude. Mrs. Tude discovered that! But it can be done with effort and hard work! So don't be lazy and let ole Atta Tude run wild. Get that boy under control!

Valu-Soup No. 8—Introducing Mr. Will Power

Will Power is a determined and braggadocios fellow. He is always telling people what he is "going to do." He is going to quit smoking, lose weight, get a better job, spend more time with his children, keep his garage clean, write his mother more often, quit watching so much TV, and on and on.

The way Will Power talks, he is going to make himself into an all but perfect human being. But talk is as far as Will Power ever gets. Oh, he changes for a few days, but then he is always right back like he was.

What is Will Power's problem? Why can't he bring about effective, long-term changes in his behavior? Some people would say that Will doesn't really want to change, but they don't know Will. He really does want to improve himself and he really does try—he tries every diet that comes along!

Is there any hope for Mr. Will Power? Yes there is! Someone has said: "When the will power and the imagination are at odds, the imagination almost always wins!" (When you think about and vividly imagine a delicious piece of pie that is in your kitchen and your will power says, "Don't you eat that pie!" what usually happens? Truthfully?)

Most people will agree that their will power is weaker than their imagination, yet when they try to improve themselves, what do most people do? They call on Mr. Will Power. And Will tries very hard to help them, but he usually fails. That leads to reduced self-value—depression, defeat and the acceptance of a lower quality of life.

But when Mr. Will Power fails to change your outward behavior, you are not defeated! Your behavior comes from your thoughts and imaginations. As someone has said: "You are what you think about all day long."

Instead of trying to force changes in your behavior, change your thoughts and mental images! Then your outward behavior will change naturally. Mr. Will Power tries to change behaviors—and produces little real results. But persistently changing your thoughts and mental images will change your life forever.

Valu-Soup No. 9—The Old Prospector

The old prospector swung his pick again. Crack! Pieces of rock flew through the air. He knelt on one knee and began to carefully handle each piece. Nothing but common stone.

How many tons of rock had he broken in thirty years of prospecting? Those years of looking for "gold in them thar hills" were beginning to show on his sun baked body. He swung his pick again. Crack! More rock; no gold.

How many times had he come up empty handed? Oh, he had found a little gold, enough to get by, but he believed there was a big strike waiting somewhere in those hills.

Other prospectors had worked that area, too, but many had drifted away. They had lost their dream. Gold fever is what they called it; that burning desire that could cause a man to leave all he had and spend years roaming through lonely, unsettled areas; chipping, digging, raking, panning, searching for the hidden treasure!

The old prospector knew of a few people who had struck it rich. They now lived in palaces in San Francisco. They had kept at it until they found gold and now they were basking in wealth and abundance.

He swung his pick again. Crack! So many folks had just given up and walked away, but he never would. He would find gold or he would die swinging that pick. Crack!

A person is not defeated until he quits trying; until he lets his dream die. Crack! Great things are accomplished through hard work, desire, determination, and persistence. Crack!

There is a greater treasure than gold! Crack! Self-value—inner peace, joy, contentment, happiness, confidence, worglee, victory over negative thoughts and painful images! Crack!

Some people have persisted in life until they made the big strike and personally experienced their championship value as a human being. Crack! A great many folks, however, have wearied of the search. Some have quit altogether–turned in their pick. Other people, although they have given up inside, still carry their pick around on their backs, so other people will think they haven't given up. A few people, like the old prospector, are still in the lonely places searching and digging to fully experience their value. Crack! They won't give up until they strike it big! Which are you?

Crack! A shout rings out! Then a series of whoops and yells! There is no one to see as an old man dances on a hillside, shouting at the top of his lungs," Gold! Gold! Hallelujah! There really is lots of gold!"

Valu-Soup No. 10–Po Tential

"Dat baby looks like somethin' the dogs done drug up!" Marcell Ledhead said, slapping his leg. "Why my lil girl has a better looking corn-shuck doll!" All of the neighbors were laughing. Ole Blue was howling.

Finis and Minnie Tential hung their heads. Their first "young un" but their friends and "kin folk" in Deep Valley were right. He really did look "poorly."

"What's y'all gonna call de lil thing?" Marcell yelped.

"Well, seeings how we's so po and de lil one, he looks so poely. I reckon we's 'ill call him 'Po.' Yessir. His name is Po Tential!"

Po was always small for his age, even though he could eat his fill of possum and "sweet-taters." He was awkward and timid, and always the object of ridicule and teasing by other children. Po spent most of his time alone. He trembled when he had to talk to anyone other than his "Ma and Pa."

When he started to school (Finis insisted that his boy was going to "get a education.") Po would come home almost every afternoon crying. By some miracle he survived twelve years of being teased and shunned.

His class graduation picture tells the story: thirty-one proud, happy teenagers and Po, shoulders stooped and looking at the floor. Most of his classmates got jobs or went into the military, but Po just stayed home and took long walks in the back woods.

One day he met a hunter. "Sorry to bother you, Sir. I reckon I'll be on my way," Po trembled.

"No please sit down," the stranger said. "I would like to talk to you. You look discouraged and defeated. What is your name?"

"Po, Sir. Po Tential."

"What a fantastic name!" the man replied.

"But Sir," Po protested. "Po means not getting enough vittles and money, and being weak and sickly."

"But Po Tential, that's a different story," the stranger said smiling. "Potential means the possibility of becoming someone great! And you have potential if I ever saw it!"

As the hunter turned to leave, Po noticed scars on his hands and forehead. And he remembered a "Bible readin'" he had learned in Sunday School: "I can do all things through Christ who strengthens me."

After that Po Tential left Deep Valley. He became a salesman, a successful business owner, a motivational speaker, and an author. His book, *Seeing Me As I Can Be*, has sold more copies than Norman Vincent Peale's, *The Power Of Positive Thinking*.

Po likes to say: "If I think about me the way others see me, that's how I'm going to be. But if I see me through the eyes of the Man from Galilee, I'll fulfill my potentiality!"

He also likes to say: "My life was rearranged when my attitude changed—now Po ain't po no mo!" And he loves to tell people: "Your potential's showing! Make it happen!"

Valu-Soup No. 11— From Air Ball To Dead-Eye

"Way to go! That's number nine! Now come on. Concentrate! You can do it!"

Air Ball Willie stood at the charity line. Never in his life had he hit 10 free throws in a row. In fact, before this time he had never even hit four in a row. And now—one more basket—and he would have 10!

Willie dribbled once and shot. SWISH! "Way to go, Willie!" coach Possa Bill jumped off the bleachers pounding the air with his fists and yelling for joy! "All right, Willie! I knew you could do it!"

"I did it, Coach! I really did it!" Willie was shouting and jumping!

"That's right! You're not 'Air Ball' any more! You've proven that to yourself! And you're not going to shoot 20 percent from the free throw line any more! No Sir, Dead-Eye Willie! You're at least an 80 percent man now!"

"Thank you, Coach!" Willie felt new confidence. And that season an amazing thing happened. Dead-Eye Willie averaged an amazing 83 percent from the line.

Coach Possa Bill was a miracle worker of sorts. He specialized in helping athletes improve their weakest areas by helping them experience and believe in their personal value and skills. And he got dramatic results!

He called his secret techniques "Possa Bill's Steps To A Way-To-Go Attitude." And he always got huge fees for his services.

But now, in order to benefit not only athletes, but anyone whose performance is hindered by a lack of self-value, his priceless secrets have been released to the general public.

And so, for the first time in book form, here are "Possa Bill's Steps To a Way-To-Go Attitude."

1) Lift high the corners of your mouth and keep them up through thick and thin! Eventually this will cause your spirit to soar. But if you let them droop, your spirit and confidence will turn sour. There is much more to a smile than just its face value.

2) Dwell on your successes, no matter how few or how small. Relive them. Savor them! Visualize them! Repeat them over and over in your mind. Then repeat them and multiply them in reality!

3) Don't relive your defeats or hurts, no matter how many or how big! Don't suffer them again and again in your thoughts. Refuse to let your defeats eat up your perception of your value. Put defeat under your feet! Stomp it! Grind it! And kick your fears in their rears!

4) Enjoy life. Pretend you are a knight of King Arthur's Round Table: Sir Laugh-a-lot!

5) Keep a clear conscience. A guilt trip is a dead end street and a value stealer. Live right and when you do wrong ask for forgiveness. Guilt will turn your confidence into "confi-dents."

6) Set moral and noble goals. Determine to reach them. Dream about them. Begin to act as if you had already achieved them. Feel confidence and value growing in your soul!

7) Trust in God. Then no matter what happens you won't need to panic. Remember that without faith, circumstances become "circum-chances" and Lady Luck is not a lady.

Now come on! You can do it! Nothing is impossible when you follow Coach Possa Bill's plan and keep a "Way-to-go attitude!"

Steve Simms

"*To be successful, you have to believe you can change the conditions in your life.*"

Buck Rogers

"*Men often conquer difficulties because they feel they can. Their confidence in themselves aspires the confidence of others.*"

Samuel Smiles

Chapter 13

Bunker Bean And The Value Of Belief

A Little Known American Novel

I'D LIKE TO TELL you about a little known American novel. It is called *Bunker Bean* and was written by Harry Leon Wilson in 1912.

Bunker Bean is the story of a man who was tricked into believing in his value. Because of his faith in his personal value, Bunker Bean achieved great success; even though his belief in his value was based on a deception.

The Story of Bunker Bean

Bunker Bean was a pitiful valu-blinder who had suffered many hardships. His parents died when he was a child and he was left on his own. People made fun of him. The author says he "roamed the earth in rags and lived timidly through its terrors." Bunker Bean was overwhelmed with fear. He was afraid of policemen, elevators, the future, various objects, social situations, and even afraid of himself.

One day he met a fake spiritualist who gave him a book on reincarnation and gradually persuaded Bunker Bean to believe in past lives. The spiritualist told Bunker Bean that for a fee, he would tell Bunker who he was before this life. Bunker jumped at the chance and paid the sum.

With great drama, the medium pretended to see a past life for Bunker Bean. He told Bunker that before this life he had been Napoleon, the great French general and Emperor.

Bunker was amazed. He asked the spiritualist how he could possibly have been Napoleon since Napoleon was so powerful and brave and he, Bunker Bean, was so weak and fearful. The make-believe medium told him that there were life cycles and that Napoleon had lived on the top part of the life cycle where the characteristics of courage, initiative, and power had been prominent. Bunker Bean, however, had lived on the bottom part of the life cycle and had the opposite characteristics.

The medium told Bunker that he had some great news—that the bottom part of the life cycle was finished and that he was about to enter the part of the life cycle that he had lived in as Napoleon. Bunker was told that he would soon feel new power and new life growing within him. Of course, none of this was true, but the spiritualist was so convincing, Bunker believed it all.

Bunker Bean Believed In His Value As A Championship Human Being

From that moment on, he began to see himself differently—he began to see himself as a person of championship value! He went to the library and read every book he could find on Napoleon so he could learn more about his supposed former self. The more he read about Napoleon, the more Bunker Bean became determined to develop Napoleon's great qualities in his life!

He found pictures of Napoleon and put them around his apartment. He constantly tried to imitate Napoleon's appearance, confidence, and attitude. Whenever he was faced with a decision or problem, he would ask himself, "What would Napoleon have done?"

One book said that Napoleon "had won his battles in his tent." So Bunker Bean decided to plan his life, just like Napoleon did and leave nothing to chance. Since there were no wars to fight, Bunker decided to use his tremendous abilities in business. What he had once done on the battle field as a great general, he would now do in business.

As Bunker continued to work and to develop the qualities of Napoleon, his life began to change. People began to notice him in a positive way. He got a promotion at work and even got a raise. Over the next few years, he became amazingly successful and happy.

Finally, one day, he found out that his friend, the make-believe medium, had tricked him for his money. Bunker had not really lived before. He was not Napoleon. He had believed a lie.

But Bunker's belief in his amazing, personal value had motivated him to work hard on doing and being the things that make for success and happiness. Even though he had believed a falsehood, his hard work and faith in himself had paid off. He may not be Napoleon, but he was indeed, a championship human being.

Bunker learned that "believing is all that matters." Later he visited the tomb of Napoleon. As tears filled his eyes, Bunker Bean was moved by the victorious secret that we have been exploring in *Your Sperm Won*, written 85 years after Harry Leon Wilson wrote *Bunker Bean*. The victorious secret as Bunker Bean put it, is that "every man is born a king." Bunker said: "Every man is born to riches." "To believe is all that matters."

A Real-Life Bunker Bean

Victor Seribriakoff is a real-life Bunker Bean. As a child his teachers thought he would never finish school. People had little faith in his ability to provide for himself.

As an adult Victor became an itinerant and worked odd jobs for years. At age thirty-two an evaluation showed Victor Seribriakoff to be a genius. He wondered how that could be possible, but then again, the written results proved he was a genius–his IQ was 161.

The proof was hard to deny, so Victor believed he was a genius and experienced an amazing transformation. He began to live, perform, and act like a genius. He wrote, invented, and got involved with several successful businesses.

Victor Seribriakoff was eventually elected chairman of the International Mensa Society–a group that requires an IQ of 140 or more for membership. Like the fictional Bunker Bean, the real-life Victor Seribriakoff vividly illustrates the power of belief.

Bunker Bean Experienced His Value

Abraham Maslow said: "The history of mankind is the history of people selling themselves short." Bunker Bean got beyond that. He believed in himself and his self-belief produced a tangible experience of his personal value.

You, Too, Have Been Tricked

Of course you're not like Bunker Bean, but you have been tricked. Bunker Bean is a fictional character. You are real and alive. Bunker Bean was tricked by a false medium, into believing in his value. You have been tricked by lying feelings, into believing in your lack of personal value.

132

Bunker Bean in his deception was closer to the truth than most of us are. Sure human beings don't recycle on earth. Napoleon is dead, never to live on our planet again. But Bunker Bean personally experienced the truth, that as a human being he has great potential, power, and value. He didn't just know it intellectually, but he lived it. And the truth of his value (even though it was based on a trick) dramatically transformed his life.

Live—Experience Your Value!

You are not and never were—a statistic! You are not and never were—a number or a series of numbers! You are not and never were—a piece of tissue! You are not and never were—a nobody! You are not and never were—good for nothing! You are not and never were—insignificant! You are not and never were—worthless! You are not and never were—only worth 98 cents when broken down to your lowest chemical level! You are not and never were—what you eat! You are not and never were—in the way! You are not and never were—a worry! You are not and never were—just a "whatever!" You are not and never were—supposed to be seen and not heard! You are not and never were—worthless!

Any of those statements that you have been called by others are LIES! And any of those things you have said to yourself are LIES! Bunker Bean finally got beyond the lies. How about you?

Move on! Move on to the truth. You are magnificent. Not because you are the so-called reincarnation of a famous dead person. You are magnificent because you are a human being—a statistical miracle. You are awesome. Believe the truth about yourself! Paul of Tarsus said: "Fight the good fight of faith (belief)."

Fighting To Believe

Mental impressions lead to beliefs. What you continually impress on your mind or allow others to vividly impress on your mind will eventually be believed by you. The only really effective way to change your beliefs is to work the source, your impressions. Your present belief system and behavior patterns are the result of hundreds of thousands of impressions made on your mind over all the years of your life.

It took a long time to develop your belief system and it will probably take a while to change it. But if you will continually change your mental impressions today, down the road your beliefs will change.

The most important mental impression maker in your mind, is your own thinking. Many people are overly concerned with the impression they make on other people, but are very careless about the mental impressions they make on themselves through harmful thinking.

Today's mental impressions are the seeds of tomorrow's beliefs. Unfortunately, many people hang out their mind like a piece of fly paper and let it collect every impression that lands on it. (No wonder they believe so many painful and self-destructive lies.)

Harmful mental impressions are everywhere, but you don't have to accept them! Instead you can fight the fight of belief! You can choose which mental impressions to accept as credible and helpful and which ones to reject as harmful trash!

A Choice Of Beliefs

For example, you're at home alone. It's dusk. There is an unexpected rap on your door! The knob begins to jiggle! Who is it? Your choice of what to believe will determine how you feel about that knock!

If you just read a newspaper story that said an escaped murderer is loose in your town and you believe that he has just looked you up to add you to his criminal record, you will feel horrified and want to hide.

However, if your spouse has been out of town and you have really missed him (or her), and you believe he has returned early to surprise you, then you will be very happy and rush to the door with love and enthusiasm.

Joy or fear in response to a door knock! Does the person who is at your door determine your attitude? No way! So far you don't really know for sure who is at your door. You just have a belief about that knock and your belief determines how you feel! (Did you get that? Your belief determines how you feel!) Believe it's a friend—feel good. Believe it's a foe—feel bad.

Jesus Christ (along with the fictional Bunker Bean) said: "As you have believed, so shall it be done unto you." In other words, you attract what you expect—what you believe.

Beliefs Are Habits Of Thought

Beliefs are habits of thought. Regularly hold a thought (an impression) in your mind and eventually it will become a belief. Keep planting, watering, and fertilizing good thoughts in your mind. Weed out the bad ones. Stick to it all summer with the persistence and determination of a championship gardener and come fall, you will have established a crop of powerful, productive beliefs!

Almost anybody can change hurtful and limiting beliefs. It just takes consistent mental hard work. The statement "I can't change" is a lie, a false belief—an excuse for low self-value.

Thought Stopper

Use the amazing "Thought Stopper!" (Not available in stores.) Gail Grumble of Grim Gulch, Wyoming says: "With 'Thought Stopper' I have been able to put our economic problems out of my mind. And if you think it's bad in other places, you ought to visit Grim Gulch! Nowadays I just keep believing that things will somehow work out. And they do! With 'Thought Stopper' I believe I could be perfectly happy, even on a desert island!"

Thank you, Gail.

Now listen to Rhonda Rude: "I just love my 'Thought Stopper.' Using it I have actually been able to quit believing bad things about people. Both of my friends now say I am actually beginning to compliment them. They can hardly believe the change in me!"

Keep up the good work, Rhonda, and before long you will have many friends.

Paul Pity says: "I used to count my problems before I fell asleep at night and I had ulcers. Now I count my blessings and eat tacos! I owe it all to 'Thought Stopper!' "

Keep on counting, Paul.

Ladies and gentlemen, you too can gain total and complete control of your thought life and of your beliefs with the incredible "Thought Stopper!" (Not available in stores.)

Now get your pen and paper ready because I am going to tell you an astonishing fact! Here it is: "Thought Stopper" is standard equipment on championship human beings (which you are if you are reading these lines). That's right. It came with you when you were born!

But. . . "Thought Stopper" must be used regularly or it soon becomes weak and ineffective. So to help you pull your "Thought Stopper" out of the proverbial drain of disuse and put it back into action stomping out painful thoughts and eliminating harmful beliefs, here are a few words from your manufacturer.

"Let not your thoughts trouble you." "Commit your works unto the Lord and your thoughts shall be established." "Bringing into captivity every thought..." "Think no evil."

So put your "Thought Stopper" to work! (Not available in stores.) And stop harmful thoughts and beliefs. Squash those things before they have time to grow. You'll feel much better and so will everyone around you.

The next time any unpleasant thought comes to mind, forcefully think the word "Stop!" The unwanted thought will leave. If it comes back drive it away again and again! Harmful thoughts cannot stay in your mind if you won't let them! That is the wonderful miracle of "Thought Stopper." (Not available in stores.) Try it! It works!

No Tricks

I cannot trick you into believing in your personal value the way Bunker Bean was tricked. But once Bunker realized he had been tricked, he had a choice. He could have returned to his pitiful and negative beliefs about himself but instead he continued to believe that he was an extremely valuable human being. After the trick, Bunker Bean had worked hard to establish and maintain his self-belief, so he had too much time and effort invested to give it up.

You have read most of this book. You have heard a lot about your overwhelming value as a championship human being. You've worked hard to stay with me this far. Now you have a choice. You can stop working and be the same way you were before you picked this book up. You can go back to believing you are just average or worse. But I hope you don't! Instead, I hope you make the choice to believe the wonderful truth about yourself!

You have heard of great battles and great victories in history. Now you know about the great battle your championship sperm fought to win the great victory of being united with your incredible egg to produce the outstanding person called you! Believe it! Believe it! I say BELIEVE IT!

"We are our own prophets for we constantly project our future state by the seeds we plant in the present."
Cheryl Canfield

"I believe that man is infinitely potential, and that given the proper guidance there is hardly a task he cannot perform or a degree of mastery in work and love that he cannot obtain."
Joshua Loth Liebman

Chapter 14

The Positive Power Of Country Music — Put Some Steam Into Your Refried Dreams

Country Music Is Often Negative

I LIVE IN THE NASHVILLE, Tennessee area so I hear a lot of country music and I like it–for the most part. But when I find myself in the shower singing "I'm going through the Big D and I don't mean Dallas," that's taking things a little too far. I mean, I don't want that–a divorce (or for country fans a D-I-V-O-R-C-E.) I am happily married and I want to stay that way. But sometimes I find myself saying and singing negative things that I don't want to happen.

Could that be because of the influence of country music? After all, much of it is negative. For example, a few years ago there was a country song that said: "You're the reason the kids are ugly, little Darling." Now that's negative. How would you like your spouse to put that one on you?

Someone once told me about a country title called "You've Left Me So Many Times It's A Wonder You're Not Gone." Pretty negative. Johnny Carson said that his favorite country song title was "I'd Rather Have A Bottle In Front Of

Me Than A Frontal Lobotomy." And who wouldn't, given those two choices.

A few years ago I picked up *The Tennessean*, the Nashville morning paper, and discovered a remarkable headline. It read something like: "Warning, Country Music Can Be Hazardous To Your Health." Now that's an amazing headline to be in a Nashville newspaper, so I read the article.

It said that research done by two university professors had shown that cities that play more country music on their radio stations have higher suicide rates than other cities. The article even gave a suicide prevention number. So I guess the moral is, if you are going to listen to country music, don't have a loaded gun or any pills nearby.

To be fair the article quoted someone from the Country Music Association saying that it wasn't country music that was causing this, but life in general. I didn't find their response too comforting.

Play It Backwards

Every time I talk about country music in my speeches and seminars, someone comes up afterwards and asks me: "Have you heard the joke about what you get if you play country music backwards?" Of course you know what you get: You get your spouse back. You sober up. You get out of prison.

A guy once interrupted one of my speeches and yelled from the back of the room: "Your dog comes home!"

Country Music Is A Metaphor For Real Life

I use country music as a metaphor for the negative ideas we have to face everyday. They come from other people, our environment, the media, and from our own mind. Like country music, negative thoughts can ring through our minds when we are in the shower, or driving, or doing whatever. But if we would begin to play our country music (our negative thoughts) backwards, we could produce good in our lives—good thoughts, good ideas, good feelings, good relationships, good times. Now that's putting some steam into your refried dreams!

"Living On Refried Dreams"

If we persistently destroy our experience of our value by playing negative thoughts and images in our mind, we will eventually be like the country song that says: "I'm messed up in Mexico, living on refried dreams." And life can do that to people. The so-called "daily grind" can rob us of our dreams.

One way to play your country music backwards and to restore your experience of your personal value is to dare to dream again!

Dream, Dream Believer

In my speeches I sometimes hold up an eight and one-half by eleven piece of cardboard and ask the audience: "How many of you believe I can cut a hole in this piece of cardboard big enough for (an audience member, let's say Reba Tillis) to walk through? Please raise your hand." Very few hands go up.

Then I ask: "How many of you don't believe I can cut a hole in this piece of cardboard big enough for Reba Tillis to walk through?" A lot of hands go up.

Finally, I ask: "How many don't care?" A few people raise their hands and enthusiastically wave them about. (It's almost as if they are saying, "I'm apathetic and I'm excited about it.")

I then set up the following proposition. If I cut a hole in this eight and one-half by eleven piece of cardboard big enough for Reba Tillis to walk through, I will have done something that many of you thought to be impossible. And if I do one thing you believe to be impossible and prove that it is possible, could there not be dozens of things about yourself that you believe to be impossible that are indeed possible? Is that possible?

At this point, most people in my audiences look confused for a few seconds and then smile and nod affirmatively. So I begin to cut and while I am cutting I talk about Christopher Columbus and how he had to have a dream and a strong belief in the possibility of a successful voyage or he would have stayed home in mediocrity.

If you don't believe in yourself and your possibilities you'll live your entire life without ever even knowing or experiencing a fraction of your value.

After I cut for awhile, a large hole opens up in that eight and one-half by eleven piece of cardboard and it is indeed big enough for Reba Tillis to walk through. In fact, I usually ask Reba (or whoever the audience member is) to come up and step through it. The audience usually applauds because they know they have seen what they had thought, only moments before, to be impossible.

Like The Song Says: "Truth Is, We're Living A Lie"

Our limiting and false beliefs cause us to live a lie. We don't dream because we don't believe we can achieve it. We don't try because we believe our efforts are useless. We settle for mediocrity because we believe that is all we deserve.

Why? Why do people believe my hole in the card proposition to be impossible? It is because they look at the cardboard and see that it is eight and one-half by eleven and then they look at Reba Tillis and see that although she is not huge, she is definitely bigger than eight and one-half by eleven. Their minds then falsely conclude that a person cannot walk through a hole in something that is smaller than he is. They come to this false conclusion because they are looking at the perceived limits—eight and one-half by eleven. Truth is, looking at the limits causes them to believe and live a lie.

"I'd Rather Be Picked Up Here Than Put Down At Home"

Look beyond the supposed limits. Don't be put down at home, especially by your own false beliefs! Instead, be picked up here and now—be encouraged. An eight and one-half by eleven piece of cardboard can be made to expand—big enough for Reba Tillis or anyone else to walk through! Your so called limits can be made to expand.

You are too valuable to be bound by false beliefs. Break through. Put some steam into your refried dreams. Dare to dream again!

A Cold, Cruel World

When I was in college I sold books door to door for three summers for the Southwestern Company. It was quite a painful experience at the time. I discovered that most people don't like someone knocking on their door and trying to sell them something. The negative responses I received (slamming doors, harsh words, negative attitudes) forced me to work on my self-value. In order to survive those summers I had to make myself play the country music backwards.

Before each summer the company held a week long "sales school." The closing speaker at the school each summer was a man named Mort Utley. He was one of the most inspirational speakers I have ever heard. After listening to him, I believed I could sell sand in the desert. Each year, Mort gave exactly the same speech. Every time I heard it I was energized and valu-ized. My favorite story that Mort told was about a 25 cent dog.

A 25 Cent Dog

Here's the story in my own words. A business man in a large city used to take the subway to work. One day, on the way to work, in the hot summertime, he noticed a small boy. The boy had a dirty, ugly dog sitting on a table, and a hand written sign that read: "Dog For Sale—25 Cents."

That evening as the man came up out of the subway he noticed the boy was still there. For the next few days, every morning and evening he saw the boy and his dog. Finally, one morning, the man stopped and said to the boy: "Son, you look like you're having a hard time selling that dog. Would you like some advice?"

"Sure!" said the little boy.

"Well, Son, there are two things you need to do. Number one; you're not thinking big enough," the man said. "People are going to value you according to the value you set. Now, no one wants a 25 cent dog—so raise your price. Believe in yourself and in your dog. Then you will sell it."

"And number two;" the man said. "Do what you can with what you have. Take that dog home and give him a bath. Comb his hair and put a nice ribbon around his neck. And make a better sign."

"Thank you, Sir!" said the boy. He packed up his table and his dog and headed off.

That evening when the man came out of the subway, he noticed the boy had taken his advice. He saw a clean, beautiful dog with a nice ribbon. There was a beautiful new sign that read: "Dog For Sale—Ten Thousand Dollars."

Have you ever over motivated someone? That's how the man felt. "Son!" he said, "I am glad you followed my advice, but there's no way you can sell your dog for ten thousand dollars!"

The boy replied: "Mister, you told me to think big and that is the biggest number I can think of. So I am going to sell my dog for ten thousand dollars."

The boy was so strong in his belief, the man didn't want to de-motivate him. So he went on home.

The next morning on the way to work, the man noticed the boy was gone. He found the sign laying in the grass. It had been marked out and "Sold" was written across it.

The man decided this was worth being late for work, so he knocked on some doors and finally found the boy's apartment. "Son," he said, "I see you've sold your dog. Do you mind if I ask you how much you got for it?"

"Ten thousand dollars," the boy said.

"Now I know you have sold him, because he's gone and I saw your new sign in the grass. But please tell me, what did you really get for him?"

"Really, Mister! I got ten thousand dollars!" the boy declared.

"How in the world did you get ten thousand dollars for a dog?" the man asked.

The boy blurted out: "I took two five thousand dollar cats for him!"

A Silly Story

Now that is a silly story. But let me ask you a question. Would you rather be in the hot sunshine with a 25 cent dog, or home in the air conditioning with two five thousand dollar cats?

I think you will agree with me that the boy got what he wanted. He got value. He got results.

Children dare to dream. My five year old daughter wants to be an astronaut, a princess, a doctor, a mother, and a window washer. She doesn't even think about limits or impossibility. She naturally plays her country music backwards. The other day she told me: "Daddy, when I grow up I sure am going to have a lot to do."

A great many adults seem to have lost their capacity to dream. How about you? Dreaming is a value increaser. You are too valuable to be stuck where you are now in life. You are too big for the place you now occupy. You are destined to grow, to expand, to accomplish. So learn to dream. Drop the limits. Reach for your future.

Like the gentleman told the little boy: Raise your price! People will value you according to the value you place on yourself. Raise your price by dreaming big dreams.

Thoughts About Dreams

Benjamin Mays said: "The tragedy of life doesn't lie in not reaching your goal. The tragedy lies in having no goal to reach. It isn't a calamity to die with dreams unfulfilled, but it is a calamity not to dream." Eleanor Roosevelt said: "The future belongs to those who believe in the beauty of their dreams."

Harry Kemp said: "The poor man is not he who is without a cent, but he who is without a dream." Louisa May Alcott said: "Far away there in the sunshine are my highest aspirations. I may not reach them, but I can look up and see their beauty, believe in them, and try to follow where they lead."

Bill Copeland said: "The problem with not having a goal (dream) is that you can spend your life running up and down the field and never scoring."

Six Steps To Put Some Steam Into Your Dream

How's your dream life? Do you have a goal, a vision? When you get out of bed in the morning do you experience your tremendous value because you are motivated by an important mission? Do you have a worthwhile purpose in your life?

Theodore Munger said: "A purpose steadily held trains the faculties into strength and aptness." In other words, it increases your experience of your value. Ray Palmer said: "One of the first conditions of success in life is a settled purpose which is to shape the whole."

So what is your purpose? Why do you get out of bed in the morning? Find, develop, and fine tune your dream and purpose with these six steps.

1) Conceive Your Dream

What do you want? If there were no limits what would you want? If you knew you couldn't fail, what would you want to do? Go ahead and express it. Take some time to think about it. Is there anything you want to do or be? Conceive it. A dream begins with a single thought.

2) Retrieve Your Dream

Don't let a newly conceived dream escape you. Retrieve it. Write it down before you forget. Cultivate it. Paint a word picture of your dream. Then paint a mental picture. Daily review your written dream. Help it grow and expand—first on paper, then in reality.

3) Believe Your Dream

Without belief dreams soon die. Why can't your dream happen to you? You came from a championship sperm and an incredible egg. You deserve to reach your dream as much as anyone else on the planet does. Believe as I have said many times in this book—believe your dream!

4) Relieve Doubt And Fear From Your Dream

Doubt and fear are dream dumpers. If you continue to entertain doubt and fear they will dump your dream out of your mind and heart. Relieve doubt and fear with faith and worglee!

5) Receive Encouragement For Your Dream

Get your hopes up. Read about people who achieved their dreams. You can too. Read self-help books. Listen to tapes.

Get away from dream stealers—"can't-do-it" people. Look for facts to support your dream. Combat wimpy feelings that tell you it is impossible. Be an encouragement engineer—build a mind set of positive expectation. Ignore set backs. Get up and go again.

6) Achieve Your Dream

You will do what you really want to do. If you work persistently hard to follow the first five steps you will eventually achieve your dream. If you continually fill your dream with steam, sooner or later the steam will propel you forward to the prize. When you really want your dream— want it with all your heart—you will get it. Desire is the fire that burns in the furnace of achievement.

Steve's Dream Steaming Questionnaire

Take some time to thoughtfully fill out this question-naire. Then read it every day for the next month. As you do, you will be programming your subconscious mind to seek these objectives.

DECIDE SPECIFICALLY WHERE YOU WANT TO GO

1) What emotions do you want to feel most often?
A)_____
B)_____
C)_____.
2) Who do you most want to be like?
A)_____
B)_____
C)_____.
3) What do you most enjoy?
A)_____
B)_____
C)_____.
4) What do you want to do that you've never done before?
A)_____
B) _____
C) _____.
5) Who, besides yourself, do you most want to see succeed and be happy in life?
A) _____
B)_____
C) _____.
6) What do you most want to be remembered for?
A) _____
B) _____
C) _____.
7) If you could be known as an expert in three areas, what would they be?
A)_____
B) _____
C) _____.

8) What do you want to do again?

A) _____

B)_____

C) _____.

9) What specifically can you do to reach these objectives? (List 10 or more specific activities that will bring you closer to these desires.)

     1)
     2)
     3)
     4)
     5)
     6)
     7)
     8)
     9)
     10)

10) List 10 or more reasons that support your belief that you can accomplish these objectives.

     1)
     2)
     3)
     4)
     5)
     6)
     7)
     8)
     9)
     10)

"Our supreme goal should be a state of mind in which invisible things are of more importance than the visible."
Alice H. Rice

"Once you know how much you matter to God, you don't have to go out and show the world how much you matter."
Mary Crowley

Chapter 15

So What Are You Really Worth?

Fair Market Appraisal

WHAT FINALLY DETERMINES THE worth of something? The value of something in a free market economic system is determined by what a willing buyer will pay for it. For example, real estate values are determined by comparing a home for sale to other homes that have recently sold in the same or in a similar neighborhood. This is called a "fair market appraisal."

So What Is Your Appraisal?

You are a human being. Has a price ever been paid for a human being similar to you? Can we find a "fair market appraisal" for you anywhere in human history?

Let's Go Back To The Roman Empire

The Romans were brutal when it came to dealing with their enemies. They used perhaps the cruelest form of execution ever known to man—crucifixion. The purpose of the

Roman cross was not just to put a man to death. There are a great many easier ways of doing that. The purpose of the cross was to bring a man extreme public shame and to cause him the greatest possible amount of physical suffering.

Crucifixion had been in occasional use among the Babylonians, Persians, Greeks, and others, but it was the Romans who made it a common means of execution. Men hanging on crosses became a familiar sight in the conquered territories of Rome.

The Romans had two methods of execution: beheading and crucifixion. Beheading was for Roman citizens and others of some social standing. Crucifixion, however, was for slaves and the lowest classes of foreigners. Roman citizens were exempt from crucifixion by law.

In order to bring about the greatest amount of shame, crucifixion was almost always preceded by scourging and mockery. Then the condemned man was made to carry the crossbeam along public roads, amidst the jeers and insults of the people, to the place of execution. He was then stripped of all his clothing and hung completely naked on the cross. A sign giving his name and sentence was put at the top of the cross and he was the object of continued mocking from people who passed by.

The physical torture of the cross was greatly increased because the process of crucifixion damaged no vital part of the human body. Death could take days! The person was attached to the cross by either tying his hands and feet to it, or by the more cruel way of nailing him to it through the wrists and feet. Thus he was held immobile, unable to cope with heat or cold and insects.

The pain of his wounds, his thirst and exhaustion, would gradually leave him so weak he could no longer support himself with his legs and he would hang limp. His body weight pulling against his arms would gradually cut off his air supply and death would come by suffocation. The process could be sped up by breaking the legs, thus causing the man to hang limp and the process of strangulation to begin.

The cross was looked upon with such horror, scandal, and loathing, that it was considered bad manners to even mention it in the presence of respectable people. The Roman Cicero said: "Let even the name of the cross be kept away, not only from the bodies of the citizens of Rome, but also from their thought, sight, and hearing." To go to the cross meant to receive the greatest possible reproach, shame, and torture!

Then one day a carpenter from Nazareth was crucified and instead of bringing shame, his death conquered the cross! Early in the fourth century the Roman Emperor Constantine banned the practice of crucifixion, in honor of Jesus Christ.

Jesus took the cross, the cruelest of all human implements and made it a universal symbol for the love of God for human beings! Now you know the best of the story!

The Best Of The Story

So what was it all about—the execution of a little known carpenter in an out of the way corner of the Roman Empire? The answer to that question shouts the infinite value of human beings louder than anything ever done, written, or spoken in human history.

The One Whose Sperm Didn't Win

According to his own statements and to the teachings of his friends and associates, Jesus Christ was no ordinary human being! He was a human being who was at the same time the Creator of the Universe. He was God in a human body.

Even today, 2000 years later, all of the world-wide followers of this carpenter (as diverse as they are) agree on some basic truths! Russian Orthodox, Roman Catholic, Presbyterian, Baptist, Pentecostal, Lutheran, Greek Orthodox, Coptic, Quaker, Charismatic, The Church of England, Methodist, non-denominational, and every other brand of Christian, officially agree on certain things!

1) Jesus Christ was fully God and fully a person. While he was a real human being, he was also the one true God in human form. He was unique in that he was the only human being in history whose sperm didn't win. He is the only human being who didn't come from a sperm meeting an egg. Instead, God's Spirit supernaturally bonded with the egg of Jesus' mother, Mary, and caused Jesus to be conceived. That is why the birth of Jesus is known as the Virgin Birth.

Therefore, the birth of Jesus Christ was an invasion of earth by God. Prior to Jesus, God had been distant, removed from the planet, an occasional visitor. After Jesus' birth, God was at hand, present, available to be approached directly by human beings. "Someone in the great somewhere" had become the living God in our midst!

2) Jesus did what had never before or since been done on our planet. He lived a perfect human life. He made no mistakes, broke none of God's rules. He measured up to God's standard of absolute perfection. No other human being has ever even come close to meeting God's standard for us.

Because we have all broken God's rules, no one can fully experience or know God. We are all separated from him because of our self-destructive behaviors, thoughts, and attitudes. Nothing we can ever do can bridge the gap between us and God.

In fact, we are so radically different from God and have so drastically broken his principles that we have earned his severest punishment. In God's court of absolute perfection all human beings, on our own, are condemned men and women.

3) God, our Creator, loves every human being so much that he wants them restored to an individual and personal

relationship with him. He wants them to measure up to his standards and to be free from his judgment and condemnation.

So in an ultimate act of love, God became a human being. He lived the perfect life for us, in our place. Then he demonstrated his love by giving his life on the cross to purchase us from the judgment we have earned. He suffered far more than the physical death. He took the entire weight of judgment for every wrong thought and every wrong deed ever committed by every human being to ever live on planet earth!

In other words, he took your place. All the judgment you deserve, for all your failings, wrong doings, and inappropriate thoughts, was put on Jesus Christ. All the punishment ever due you was placed on him. That is the price paid for you!

The Price Paid For You

So what are you worth? You are worth the price that a willing buyer will pay for you! And a willing buyer, God, himself, has given his life in exchange for yours! You are worth the life of God!

Think about it! Let it sink in! Who do you think you are? The greatest price ever paid for anything in the universe was paid for you! A human being could never even think of anything greater than the life of God! And God, in Jesus, gave his life for you! Talk about value! You are priceless.

Yet the reality of your value cannot be grasped by your intellect alone. It goes so much deeper than mind. It cuts to the heart, pierces the soul, apprehends the inner being. Experience your value.

Experience Your Value

4) The fourth thing that the diverse followers of Jesus agree on is victory over death! The dead Jesus came back to life three days later. His corpse got up and walked out of the tomb. Hundreds of his early followers saw him alive from the dead.

After forty days of appearing numerous times to people, Jesus, in his body drifted up to a cloud and disappeared. He had told his followers that he would send his Spirit on them, and ten days later his supernatural presence and power filled a group of his followers.

They were so radically transformed that they boldly told everyone about Jesus. Most of them were murdered for what they believed. But even physical death couldn't stop them. Their example of love and power and courage caused millions of others around the world to personally experience the living Jesus.

True value comes from that experience. Some call it being "born again," others call it conversion or "being saved." Some call it "meeting Jesus." I call it wonderful! It is really beyond words! It is a revelation—a seeing of the reality of God. It is a personal encounter with God's love.

A Personal Disclosure

I write and speak about positive thinking and self-help. I have learned many ideas and techniques of self-management that have made a profound difference in my life. I share these in my speeches and books because valuable people, like you and me, need to lift ourselves up and experience our value.

In the rest of this chapter I would like to share with you the most powerful value builder I have ever experienced.

I grew up going to church, but I was always longing for something more. Somehow an hour's worth of people half-heartedly singing a few hundred-year-old songs and then listening to a man talk, didn't do much for me. I remember one day when I sat in church as a teenager. The thought came to my mind: "If you were born a Hindu, what would you be today?" I pondered that for awhile. I realized if I had grown up a Hindu, if I had attended Hindu temple, and my parents had been Hindus, then I would have been a Hindu.

As I admitted that to myself, another thought came to my mind: "Then why do you think you are a Christian?" As I thought about it I realized that my only reason for thinking I was a Christian was because I was born in a Christian area of the world and exposed to Christian religion. That didn't seem like a good reason to me, so that very moment I rejected Christianity. I remember saying: "God, I don't believe in Jesus, please show me the truth."

A couple of years later when I was a freshman in college I stumbled into an informal meeting of sixty or so people in my dormitory. Some guy was talking to the group and telling them that he had "met Jesus Christ." As he spoke he had such enthusiasm and faith, he seemed to me to be glowing.

After he spoke, another guy told about his experience of "meeting Jesus." I had never heard that in my life. I had mistakenly believed that Jesus was only a historical figure like George Washington—dead and gone. But these guys said he was alive and available for me to experience.

Something happened to me that night! There were no trumpets or thunder or weeping or shouting, but something happened to me. I had what I believe to be an encounter with the person of Christ and that began a personal relationship with him. The experience was internal. It was supernatural. It didn't make sense to me, but it changed me completely.

I began to read the Bible, which I thought was only a religious book. Reading it was like touching an electric outlet— it was alive. I gradually began to believe the content of

Scripture, not because of religious tradition, but because it was becoming so real in my life.

Of all the sources of value and self-help I have ever used or experienced, none compare with a "meeting Jesus" experience. This experience is not something that belongs only to an individual or an institution or even to a religion or a culture. It is an experience open to everybody on the planet. If your sperm won, you can encounter the living Jesus Christ.

Life's Most Valuable Encounter

Of all the advice I give in this book, this is the most important. Talk to God—not formally or in religious language —but like you are talking to a good friend. Tell him the truth— you believe in him or you don't believe in him. He knows anyhow. Then ask him to show or reveal himself to you. Ask him to show you if Jesus Christ is really God in human form. Ask him to show you if you are really so valuable that the life of God was paid for you.

Then give him a chance to answer. Remain open. Don't close your mind and heart. If you sincerely ask him to show himself to you, the living God will do it! So ask. Then stand by and see what happens! You are about to be launched into a new dimension of value!

An unbelievable price has been paid for you—you world class, championship winner! The life of God. How valuable you are!

How Did Mother Teresa Do It

How does one person start a movement of more than 4,500 people doing free of charge and at great personal sacrifice, some of the most unpleasant and disgusting tasks known to man? Mother Teresa started taking care of the sickest, dirtiest, and lowliest people in the nation of India. She calls them "the poorest of the poor."

She would personally bathe their bodies and their wounds. Since many were dying she would take them home and let them die "with dignity" at her place. Over the years thousands joined her in this activity and now the Sisters of Charity and Brothers of Charity are world-wide movements!

Mother Teresa was awarded the Nobel Peace Prize in 1979 and the Congressional Gold Medal, the highest civilian award the United States Congress can give, in 1997. Senators Edward Kennedy and Sam Brownback wrote: "We should not miss an opportunity to learn from one of the most endearing people in modern history."

How did she do it? Here is what Mother Teresa said: "Let us keep that joy of loving Jesus in our hearts, and share that joy with all we come in touch with. That radiating joy is real, for we have no reason not to be happy, because we have Christ with us. Christ in our hearts. Christ in the poor we meet."

Mother Teresa knows the source of true value! She finds value in herself because of Christ. She also finds value in the "poorest of the poor" because of Christ. She said that her motive for such sacrificial service to the outcasts of the world is because she sees Jesus Christ in them—and her act of loving and valuing the poor is because of the value Jesus gives them. After all, even the least lovely people on the planet were paid for with the life of God! That is their true value and ours!

Steve Simms

"Once you learn how good you really are, you never settle for playing anything less than your very best."
Reggie Jackson

"What has taken over by tiny degrees must be edged out the same way. The fact that we are taking small steps does not minimize a very great commitment."
Joyce Sequichie Hifler

Chapter 16

Valu-Live--The Treasure Of You

The Truth About Yourself

SO HERE IT IS--THE TRUTH about yourself. I'm summing up this book with a statement about your value. Say it loud and say it proud. Here is "The Treasure Of You" written in the first person singular.

The Treasure Of Me

An amazing treasure has been hidden on earth--unrecognized and undiscovered for years. This extraordinary treasure has been confused with the common and the ordinary. The treasure is me.

I am a unique person who overcame impossible odds when I first appeared on this planet. Statistically my existence is impossible. I shouldn't be here--but I am. My very existence declares that I am a magnificent winner. I am an indescribable treasure--full of value! In fact, I am priceless! My worth is infinite!

All the things I see around me—all the things I or anybody else could ever own are worth nothing when compared with my value.

From this point on in my life. . . I will no longer fail to recognize and appreciate the treasure of me. I will take good care of the treasure of me and use it wisely. I will treat myself with all the love and respect due someone of unlimited value! I will avoid self-destruction and turn to self-cultivation.

I will also treasure all the other infinitely valuable human beings on the planet. I will recognize and respect the treasure of them. I will see myself as a statistical miracle living on a planet of other miracles. And I will celebrate my life and the life of others!

Because of my tremendous value, I will valu-live. My sperm won! I beat the odds! And I will beat any obstacle life may put in my way! I will continue to be a winner my whole life by recognizing and accepting my winning status as the treasure of me!

Nothing can devalue me but myself! Problems, circumstances, other people, economics, even sickness or ultimately death. Nothing can devalue me for the treasure of me is more than an accident. As Mother Teresa sees infinite value in the poorest human beings because of Christ, so I can always find value in me! And I will!

Nothing can devalue me and I choose not to devalue myself. I feel good! I celebrate! I love! I serve! I am a part of the most important enterprise in the universe—human life—made in the image of God and purchased with the life of God!

What am I worth? I can never describe my value! So instead I will experience it. I will believe it. I will treasure it. I will live it. I will pass it on to others. What an honor I have — to be alive. I am grateful for the treasure of me!

Valu-Live

Zig Ziglar asks a question: "If you had a championship race horse, how many of you would let it stay up all night, smoke cigarettes, and drink beer?" How about you? If you had a ten million dollar race horse would you let it harm itself (and your investment)? Of course not.

Let me ask you this: What makes you do things, say things, and think things that are self-destructive? The next time you are about to engage in a behavior, an attitude, or a thought that may cause yourself harm, ask yourself: "Would I do this to a ten million dollar race horse that I owned?" If you answer no, then don't do it to yourself either! After all, a ten million dollar race horse is cheap compared to you!

To value-live begin to valu-talk, valu-think, valu-serve, valu-act, valu-stand, valu-share, and valu-be.

Valu-Talk—Speak Adult Language

We live in an odd culture where the term "adult language" refers to off color, obscene, and profane language. A better name for that, however, is adolescent language.

What is real adult language? Try this on for size: commitment, love, service, value, character, honesty, integrity, faithfulness, honor, gratitude, peacefulness, purity, duty, responsibility, joy, appreciation. True adult language is valu-talk.

Observe your conversation for a day. Ask yourself: "Would a person of tremendous value talk like I do?"

Valu-Think—Program Your Mental Computer For Value

Big Blue is the IBM super computer that beat the world's chess champion. Big Blue, the world's most powerful computer, is worth a bundle! It has an extremely high value (which, however, is peanuts compared to your value).

As valuable and powerful as Big Blue is, what would happen if the programmers programmed it with faulty software, viruses, self-destructive ideas, and non-sense? How would Big Blue perform? Lousy! You and I could even beat it in chess!

Why? Because faulty and destructive programming would make it totally ineffective. It would still be valuable, but not very useful.

How about you? How's your programming--your thinking? Do you valu-think or do you devalu-think? Ask yourself: "Does the way I think build my value and effectiveness or does my thinking create limits and pain for me?"

Valu-Serve--Pass It On

Value produces opportunities to help other people. Because you are such an outstanding human being you have talents and abilities that can help the people around you. Serving is not demeaning. It is value enhancing. The more you use your gifts, not just for yourself but also for others, the more you experience your personal value.

Nothing feels better than to help somebody! Dick Gregory said: "One of the secrets I keep learning is: the secret of being happy is doing things for other people." And Abbe Pierre said: "We need to be needed. Service to others can give us a new purpose in life."

"Random Acts of Kindness" is a popular idea. But an idea is like a hand saw, it won't work unless you do. Ask yourself: "What can I do to make a difference in someone's life today?"

Valu-Act—Where The Rubber Meets The Road

Do. What do you do? How do you live your life? Would a person observing your daily behavior, your routine, determine that you believe yourself to be a valuable person? Or would a person watching you decide that you believe you are not worth much?

Anybody would treat an old nag a lot different than a ten million dollar race horse. Do you act like you are an old nag or do you act like you are a champion?

"Do" has nothing to do with feelings. Many times I feel like a nag, but I can still control what I do! Continually say this to yourself: "I may not be able to control how I feel at this moment but I can control how I act!" That is the truth! So valu-act! Pretend you are an actor playing the role of a person who originated from a championship sperm meeting an incredible egg!

Ask yourself: "Does my daily behavior demonstrate self-value or self-destruction?"

Valu-Stand—Values For The Valuable

Someone has said: "If you don't stand for something, you'll fall for anything!" What do you stand for? Do your principles illustrate your high personal value or do they indicate that you've undervalued yourself—sold yourself short?

Your belief system, your ethics, and your goals tell everyone what you think you are worth! Did you build your belief system yourself or did you absorb it from your culture, your family, your friends, the media?

As valuable human beings we live in a devalued human world. Worldwide, moral values are low. Behaviors and attitudes that people a generation or two ago would have been ashamed of, are today praised and publicly proclaimed. Ethics are low. Lying, cheating, and stealing are considered expedient. Many people intentionally enslave themselves to their lying feelings by living by the adage: "If it feels good do it!"

We've lost our heros. Today we have a lot of famous people, but very few heros! A hero is someone who believes and lives by high principles! Felix Adler said: "The hero is one who kindles a great light in the world, who sets up blazing torches in the dark streets of life for me to see by."

Remember the American patriot, Patrick Henry: "Give me liberty or give me death!" Or the German reformer, Martin Luther, who when told to change his views or be killed said: "Here I stand, I can't do anything else!"

Principles. Ask yourself: "Do I have any beliefs or principles that I would stand for even at the cost of my life? Are my principles pillars of value or are they weak and selfish?"

Valu-Share—Honoring Value In Others

How do you see other human beings? How about strangers? How about people from other races, cultures, or countries? How about people on the other side of the globe? How about the poorest person you've seen in the past year? Or the richest? How about the terminally ill? How about people who are engaging in self-destructive behaviors? How about people who dislike or hate you?

If you devalue any human life you devalue yourself! Ultimately, I am not any more valuable than anybody else on the planet. I may behave better or think better or serve more, but I am not more valuable. Therefore if I fail to recognize the value in another human being I will fail to recognize my own full value.

Now recognizing the value of a human being doesn't mean that I agree with him or approve of his behavior. It doesn't mean I don't hold people responsible for their actions.

I don't have to tolerate injustice. Even very valuable people do wrong and when they do they suffer the consequences. A person who commits an awful crime should be punished to the full extent of the law, but that doesn't mean he doesn't have ultimate value.

We live in a world full of valuable, championship human beings. Oh, they don't always act like they are valuable (neither do I, even though I try), but the value is there as I have shown in this book.

Ask yourself: "Do I valu-share? Do I believe other people are as valuable as I am?"

Valu-Be—Be What You Already Are

An apple tree doesn't work hard to produce apples. It just "be's" an apple tree and apples happen. A person is called a human being, not a human doing. Many of us, however get caught in the paradox between being and doing. We feel inadequate in who and what we are, so we try to compensate by incessant doing. The only problem is that we can never do, accomplish, or earn enough to give us an inner sense of value.

Even Elvis Presley, with as much money and fame as he achieved, couldn't find value in his outward accomplishments. Although his accomplishments live on in the hearts of tens of millions of people around the world, Elvis couldn't find enough value of being in his own heart to avoid self-destruction. Doing alone can never give ultimate value! You've got to valu-be!

Ask yourself: "Do I see my intrinsic worth as a human being? Do I experience value in just being me?" (If not, read this book again and again until you believe it! Remember Bunker Bean!)

167

The Strongest Chain

The strongest chain in the world is not made of steel or any other metal. It is made of something far more powerful than that--something that scientists don't fully understand.

The chain has a fascinating property. It is invisible to the human eye. It can't be seen, but it can be felt. And when it is used to bind someone it is far more effective than conventional chains.

Everybody who has ever lived has been bound by this chain. Very few people ever completely escape its clutches. This chain has done more harm to the human race than floods or earthquakes or famines or wars.

Because this chain is invisible, most of the people who are shackled by it sincerely believe they are free. It is easy to see the damage done to other people by this chain, but it is difficult to recognize its destructive work in your own life.

Most people blame circumstances and other people for the chain's carnage in their life. They don't realize--they just don't see--that they are bound by the chain of thought--that most of their problems occur between their own ears!

The chain of thought has many links to help it tighten and squeeze the self-value out of a person's soul. Fear, hatred, self-pity, guilt, depression, lust, pride, unforgiveness, self-doubt, prejudice, tradition, greed, unbelief; though invisible and often undetected, grip the human mind causing more pain than the chamber of horrors in the dungeon of a medieval castle.

Although the chain of thought is extremely strong, it can be broken through life-long battle. Human beings are so tangled up in the chain of thought that it is hard to distinguish between the links of the chain and our own personality.

The Key To The Chain

This book, *Your Sperm Won—Experiencing Your Value As A Championship Human Being,* has been about breaking free from the chain of thought! You can do it! Recognizing your tremendous value is the key that unlocks the chain of thought!

Although experiencing your value can begin in a moment, it takes a lifetime of seeking to fully know your worth! After reading this book you've probably understood the concepts in your head, but are they in your heart? You learned some information, but have you obtained any inspiration? Facts alone don't change lives, passion does!

Joanna Field said: "There is all the difference in the world in knowing something intellectually and knowing it as a lived experience." You deserve more than what you are now experiencing. You deserve a better life. I am not talking about money but about peace, joy, and contentment—the personal experience of your personal value! You deserve it! So go for it! Don't be satisfied to feel average, normal, or mediocre. Don't be satisfied to hurt and slowly (or rapidly) self-destruct!

Your destiny is far greater than that! You are a world class human being! You came from a championship sperm and an incredible egg! You are a somebody!

Begin now to more fully treasure the treasure of you!

The Beginning
of a Better Life . . .

Bring America's Encouragement Engineer,
Steve Simms
To Your Next Meeting!

Topics:

Don't Lose Your Marbles
Lighten Up And Succeed
The Spirit of Serving Customers
Staying Calm And Productive In Changing Times

Steve has presented speeches and seminars for associations and corporations across the nation, including:

International Association of Hospitality Accountants

National Association of Music Merchants

TelcoResearch

Florida Gift Fruit Shippers Association

National Fraternal Congress of America

International City/County Managers Association

American Society of Consultant Pharmacists

Georgia Pharmacy Association

United Cities Gas

Montana, Texas, Tennessee, New Mexico, Indiana, Mississippi, Nebraska, Arizona, and Illinois Health Care Associations

Chambers of Commerce

National Association of Police Athletic Leagues

Schools and School Boards

Colorado, Idaho, Tennessee, Iowa, West Virginia, Texas, Kansas, Michigan, Oklahoma, Arizona, and Ohio Municipal Leagues

National Health Corp. LP

A dynamic speaking style, targeted content, uplifting humor, and a warm, friendly manner make Steve Simms' keynote speeches and seminars a treat for audiences in corporations and associations nationwide.

To discuss scheduling Steve for your next meeting call:

(615) 371-8100

Steve Simms

Your Sperm Won!

Value Building Resources
From Attitude-Lifter Enterprises

Mindrobics--How To Be Happy For The
Rest Of Your Life --by Steve Simms (6 X 9 trade paperback-172 pages)

$12.95 each . . . . $_____

10 or more $10.95 each

50 or more $ 8.95 each

Mindrobics–by Steve Simms (Tape Series, 6 cassettes--5 1/2 hours)

$59.95 each . . . .$_____

Lighten Up And Succeed –

by Steve Simms (single cassette tape--approximately 45 minutes)

$10.95 each . . . .$_____

Magic Coloring Book --(see page 51 of this book)

$15.00 each . . . .$_____

Your Sperm Won—Experiencing Your Value As A Championship Human Being

by Steve Simms

$12.95 each . . . .$_____

10 or more $10.95 each

50 or more $8.95 each

SUBTOTAL $_____

TN Residents only--add 8.25% sales tax $_____

Shipping--add 5% of order ($3.00 minimum) $_____

TOTAL $_____

Mail check to: Your Name _____

Attitude-Lifter Enterprises   Address: _____

2720 Hillsboro Road   _____

Brentwood, TN 37027

(615) 371-8100 - VISA and MasterCard accepted.

Steve Simms

Improve Yourself and Your Company
With Instrumented Learning Profiles
From Carlson Learning Company

- Use individually or with groups.
- Answer questions with a coin rub.
- Gain amazing insights into your behavior.
- Develop a personalized self-improvement plan.

_____Coping & Stress Profile @ $15.00 ea.	$_____
_____Personal Listening Profile @ $13.00 ea.	$_____
_____Dimensions of Leadership Profile @ $13.00 ea.	$_____
_____Discovering Diversity Profile @ $13.00 ea.	$_____
_____Innovate with C.A.R.E. Profile @ $13.00 ea.	$_____
_____Biblical Personal Profile (DiSC) @ $13.00 ea.	$_____
_____Values Profile System @ $13.00 ea.	$_____
_____Time Management Profile @ $15.00 ea.	$_____
_____Personal Learning Insights Profile @ $13.00 ea.	$_____
_____Personal Profile System (DiSC) @ $13.00 ea.	$_____
Tennessee Residents add 8.25% sales tax	$_____
Shipping & Handling add $2.00	$___2.00___
Total	$_____

Mail Check to :
 Steve Simms
Attitude-Lifter Enterprises
2720 Hillsboro Road
Brentwood, TN 37027

Your Name:_____

Address: _____

_____

Or call for more information: (615) 371-8100
Visa and MasterCard accepted.